anitya

Gayatri Jayaraman is a mind-body-spirit therapist. She is the founder of Shamah | शमः and LOGOS | λόγος, alignment practices based in Mumbai.

PRAISE FOR THE BOOK

'Rooted in the dharma of the Buddha's Four Noble Truths, Gayatri's work is a poetic meditation that will guide you to navigate the arduous path of change in a way that almost seems organic and intuitive.'

– Amish, bestselling author of the Shiva Trilogy

'I read this book like I would read the sky, not knowing where I'd be taken next, but assured that I'd be protected by the gentle and incisive voice of the writer like the sky does, changing every moment but never falling on me. I read this book with gratitude. Gayatri Jayaraman has written a book that has given many of my unarticulated emotions the dignity of understanding.'

– Sumana Roy, author of *How I Became a Tree*

Also by the author

Sit Your Self Down: A Novice's Journey into the Heart of Vipassana

anitya

How to Make the Most of Change and Transform Your Life

GAYATRI JAYARAMAN

hachette
INDIA

First published in India in 2021 by Hachette India
(Registered name: Hachette Book Publishing India Pvt. Ltd)
An Hachette UK company
www.hachetteindia.com

1

ISBN 978-93-91028-26-8

Author photograph by Abhijit Bhatlekar

Hachette Book Publishing India Pvt. Ltd
4th & 5th Floors, Corporate Centre,
Plot No. 94, Sector 44, Gurugram – 122003, India

Typeset in Baskerville on 11/15.8
by Jojy Philip, New Delhi – 15

Printed and bound in India
by Manipal Technologies Limited, Manipal

MIX
Paper from responsible sources
FSC™ C043100

To

All who suffer
May you be free of your suffering

tārakā timiraṃ dīpo
māyāvaśyāyabudbudaṃ
svapnaṃ ca vidyudabhraṃ ca
evaṃ draṣṭavyaṃ saṃskṛtaṃ

So you should view this fleeting world
A star at dawn, a bubble in a stream,
A flash of lightning in a summer cloud,
A flickering lamp, a phantom, and a dream.

– Hui Neng
(From *The Diamond Sutra*,
translated by Bill Porter, alias Red Pine)

Author's Note

The four sections of this book are based on a meditated interpretation of Gautama Buddha's Four Noble Truths: Dukkha (Suffering), Samudaya (the Cause), Nirodha (the Cessation) and Magga (the Path), in the context of the suffering of change.

It uses the lens of mind, body and spirit counselling to achieve this. Identities in case studies have been changed or cited with permission. This guide does not claim to stand in lieu of psychological intervention. If you are suffering from anxiety or depression related to change, it is highly recommended that you seek the counsel of a trained mental health practitioner.

Author's Note

When the Dharma has not yet fully penetrated body and mind, one thinks one is already filled with it.

When the Dharma fills body and mind, one thinks something is lacking.

When we sail a boat into the ocean, beyond sight of land, and our eyes scan the four directions, it simply looks like a circle.

No other shape appears.

This great ocean, however, is neither round nor square.

It has inexhaustible characteristics.

To a fish it looks like a palace; to a heavenly being a jewelled necklace.

To us as far as our eyes can see, it looks like a circle.

All the myriad things are like this.

Within the dusty world and beyond, there are innumerable aspects and characteristics; we only see or grasp as far as the power of our eye of study and practice can see.

When we listen to the reality of myriad things, we must know that there are inexhaustible characteristics in both ocean and mountains, and there are many other worlds in the four directions.

This is true not only in the external world, but also right under our feet or within a single drop of water.

– Zen Master Eihei Dōgen

(From the *Realizing Genjokoan: The Key to Dogen's Shobogenzo*, translated by Shōhaku Okumura)

Contents

MOUNTAIN

Dukkha, the Suffering of Change

I

Gather Me My Fragments

ONCE STOOD A MOUNTAIN, SHIMMERING WITH DEPOSITS OF mica, feldspar, quartz and opal. He was clad in fine firs, sal and silver birch, the handsome angles of his rock glinting above the snowline. Eagles nested in his crevices, panthers roamed his ridges. He was a constant friend to moody clouds, lonely skies and wandering hawks. One day, a meteor, all nickel and iron, hit him in the face. The forests burned for days. When the smoke parted, the mountain was gone, crumbled into his own foothills. The skies wept and carried his sediments to the sea. Over thousands of years, as long as he had been a mountain, the undulating waves grated him down to granules of sand. He lay in bits among mollusc, bone and coral. He was trawled by motor and molten by furnace until tints long-buried emerged, bringing out hues he had forgotten lay within him. Hand-blown by artisans, he was carried gently to the footpaths of the Rialto Bridge for tourists to gawk at. He now lives – a stained-glass window in a church, in a vase, a gemstone, a pebble in a pond, a brick in a wall. At once, both, a mountain and not.

~

Change can be gentle or cataclysmic. A poltergeist, change can rearrange our furniture as we sleep. A prankster, it can pull the chair out from under us as we sit. It can creep up on us, taking years to weave a delicate web of lines across our faces. It can deliver bodily surprises, leaving us gasping for breath. Seek certainty, change mocks us. Seek to control it, it evades grasp.

We are playing a game with change in which the rules keep changing. We set goals, defend our goalposts, arrange our lives around them, and muster the courage to go on the offence. We find focus, train hard, and protect ourselves from all that detracts us. Then, change hits us like an earthquake that moves the ground beneath our feet. We were on track but now the goalpost has shifted. All progress is disrupted. It is frustrating.

We arrive at change reluctantly. Most change is involuntary while our moving on from it is required to be voluntary. This is where our wheels get stuck in the mud of the past. In the wishing that things could remain as they were. Constancy is comforting and regarded as a sign of longevity; rootedness is wholesome. We are taught this throughout our lives. In the context of our own human frailty, we actively seek such stability through the homes we build, the relationships we forge, the marriages we make, and the legacies we pass down. The only antidote to change we are told is to 'persist' and work even harder against its attempts to derail us. So, we're spending our lives in an exhausting game of chasing the shifting goalpost. Our pursuit of permanence seems interminable until it dawns on us that it is inherently fruitless. It is an endless dissatisfaction. **Dukkha, which is Suffering, exists. This is a fact. This is the Buddha's First Noble Truth. Change is a kind of suffering.**

The Buddha taught Four Noble Truths: Dukkha, Samudaya, Nirodha and Magga. These pointed out the fact of suffering, that suffering has a cause, it has an end, and there is a way out.

There are three kinds of Dukkha: Suffering of Suffering, the Suffering of Change, and All-Pervasive Suffering. The first is organic decay, degeneration, illness and death. The change that most of us grapple with in our daily lives, of things not working out as we expect them to, is the suffering of the second kind. The third is the anguish of finding purpose in our lives.

Knowing these Truths brings us to an awareness of three fundamental characteristics of our existence, i.e., the Trilakshana. These are Impermanence or Anitya, Suffering or Dukkha, and Non-Essence or Anatma. In the Anguttara Nikaya III. 134, the Buddha says:

> *Whether Perfect Ones appear in the world or not, it still remains a firm condition, an immutable fact, and fixed law that all formations are impermanent, that they are subject to suffering, and that everything is without Self.*

All formations, anything that is born, sustained, decays and dies, has these characteristics.

So, you see, Impermanence, Anitya, is not just something that happens to us, it defines us. To exist is to be impermanent. It's not just us either, but anything that is created in the world. This is a relief to know because it means that the onslaught of change is not personal. It also means our resistance to change is futile. Resisting change is almost like doing battle with our DNA – we are trying to combat one of our most fundamental attributes, which is impossible. Our lifelong quest for stability, rootedness and constancy goes against our inherent nature.

What is the difference between the change we struggle with on a daily basis and the Impermanence that is hardwired into our existence? The first is apparent in ignorance, the latter in awareness. Our journey is to move from suffering with change to gaining the equanimity of Impermanence.

To exist is to change.
We suffer from change.
Change in itself is a form of suffering.
Awareness of change is an exit from suffering.
These are all truths of change.

The good news is that the solution lies within the problem, and both are exactly the same. All we have to change is how we deal with change.

A few years ago, I listed all the houses I had lived in. I had lived in over 40 homes. While I grew up with a healthy disregard for growing roots, I also realized people internalize change differently. My siblings would manifest this in their adulthood as the urge to hunker down into stability. My rolling stone ran riot; I moved a lot. I did yearn for the infrastructure that permanence seemingly brought to others – from wall-mounted closets to childhood friends. Miranda Lambert's song *The House That Built Me* invariably makes me wrack my head to think of a house that did the same for me. Fortunately, such yearnings pass quickly when I count my freedoms: I live lightly, have little clutter and suffer no loss too deeply. I am a pebble merrily skipping across the pond of life. Adapting to change has become second nature.

It was only later in life, however, that I started viewing this adaptability as a desirable trait. Until then, I introjected the view of myself as being unable to grow roots. What no one tells us as we are urged to 'settle down' and 'compromise' in our twenties, is that the vices of our youth become the defining virtues of our adulthood. Your refusal to accept a misogynistic work situation is what turns you into the person spearheading gender equality in your later years. It just seems hard to do when you've to push past the naysayers to do it. Change is like that. For all the change you undergo in your twenties, you will find people urging you to stop, settle, adjust. Don't. The practice of embracing change happens in the face of those who make a virtue of its opposite – constancy. It's what will keep you standing when change hurtles down the lane at you and the skittles begin to fall. And it will.

From 2016 onwards, bestselling author Amish has faced one of the toughest periods in his life. Professionally, he was at his peak. His books, Raavan, Suheldev *and* Dharma *outsold all his previous bestsellers. However, personally, he lost his father-in-law and his brother-in-law, both of whom were father figures to him, and then his father too. His longstanding marriage disintegrated. He took up a new post as the director of the Nehru Centre, which took him to London, separating him from family and friends. His older brother contracted Covid-19, his mother fell ill and the pandemic kept him isolated from the anchor of his life, his son, Neel. He was isolated from all of his usual support structures. Nothing about it was good. There was no silver lining, nothing to derive from it but acknowledge the grief, loss and pain, and keep moving on. Director Shekhar Kapur urged him to tap into his emotion of pain like artists do. Amish couldn't find a way to reconcile with this. Nobody could possibly wish for such change. Kapur gently explained to him that pain beyond a point causes paralysis, and it is the paralysis, not the pain, that causes suffering. As he struggled to cope, Amish realized that Shekhar was right, and moved to accepting the pain of such far-reaching change. It began to influence his personal beliefs and value systems. A devout Shaivite with a foundational belief in seeing life as essentially* ananda *(bliss) he moved to seeing life as essentially* dukkha *(suffering). When he began to accept the dukkha, Amish says, coping with the change became easier. He could turn his focus to small points of happiness amid the pain, to value jogs in the park, reading, long chats with friends and virtual connections with family. 'When you see the suffering of change as the basis, you are able to focus not on finding happiness, but a sense of purpose. When you see how bad the bad can be, you value the goodness of the good. Change can be positive or negative. We aren't always stoic, so it's important to live by a theory of relativity and enjoy the moment,' he says.*

Embracing change sounds like the stuff of nightmares, like pretending we are all on board with it. Suffering through change is undoubtedly a terrible thing.

Say, the organization we work with lays off 100 people, many of them close friends and colleagues we've worked with for years. We know they have instalments to meet, children and ailing parents to support, dreams, goals and hopes that are now dashed. We see them afraid and losing hope. We know it could easily have been us. It probably will be in the next round of pink slips. They didn't deserve what happened to them and when it happens to us, neither will we.

Change is viscerally painful. So do we simply deny how hard it is and move on? Change is a shock to the psychological, physical and spiritual system. It inflicts violence. We resist. We feel the pain of the resistance. Who can blame us? Returning to the cocoon of the prenatal state can feel so much easier than coping with the nakedness that change delivers us into. Change is hard.

Order a coffee at a busy café. Pick a great seat by the sunny window. Halfway through the coffee, vacate your seat, taking care not to leave any personal object behind that would signify the chair as reserved in any way. Go to the counter to buy something else or head to the washroom, look at pastries in the display cabinet, walk around the café, then return to your table. If the chair is occupied, observe your reaction. Most of us display a slight purse of the lips, a wrinkle in the forehead, a slight clenching of the jawline. Observe any sensations of tightness in your stomach or chest or if your shoulders tense up. 'You think, "my" chair is gone.' Some of us might even go up to the occupant and say, 'Excuse me, you're in my chair.' Even though the chair was not 'yours' before you came into the café.

Our resistance to change is deeply ingrained and makes itself apparent across an integrated mind, body and spirit level. Our default setting is that when things start to go out of control, we work harder to try to get them under control. When the goalpost moves, we run harder towards it. When things become chaotic, we become even more organized. We may give ourselves the illusion of being in command for a while, but change is a wily fellow, always just a step ahead. A lot of our anxiety comes from attempting to control the uncontrollable and bringing the disorder to order.

As the coronavirus pandemic finishes off what the economic slowdown began, demolishing the carefully laid plans of meticulous life architects, change has become a way of life. Entire industries have collapsed, long-time employees laid off, factories and bureau offices shut, unorganized workers set into a reverse migration, and people are taking on roles they are ill-prepared for. Weddings have been postponed, admissions deferred, job offers rescinded, exam dates pushed and relocations stuck. One family sent their furniture to their new home in another state the day before borders shut. They were stuck in an emptied-out house through an ever-extending lockdown with nothing to sit or sleep on and no utensils to cook with. However, what the pandemic won't destroy, a riot, an earthquake, a flood, a loss of a supply chain link, crashing real estate prices, or rising interest rates in an already precarious economic environment will. The ground is constantly shifting under our feet. We're shouting 'excuse me, you're in my chair', but no one seems to be listening.

Anoushka Gautam was 19 when she left her cosy parental home in Dubai to join her university in Vancouver in 2019. She was nearing the end of her first year when the pandemic hit. The relocation was not just a geographic one, but a migration of mindset. She felt a range of emotions from fear and competitiveness to enthusiasm and anxiety. Hardest to come by was a sense of security. 'Moving away meant figuring out the world for myself and assimilating with different cultures and people,' she says. Her school counsellor advised her to be kinder to herself and a teacher suggested she stop working so hard and go watch a rubbish film. It took her a year to grasp these concepts. Until then, she worked on the principle that when things go out of control, you need to work even harder at controlling them.

Anoushka had lived through three phases of radical change by now – leaving school and home for college, adapting to her new life there, and dealing with the instability brought on by the pandemic. The first had proven to be the most liberating, giving her milestones to count her progress by, namely her A levels and her independence after flying the coop. The second was the scariest, as she was forced to rediscover herself, her goals and her identity. She wasn't Indian enough for the Indians in Vancouver and not foreign enough for the Canadians. She had to turn her lens inwards to find where she fit in. Bollywood songs became the familiar thread between her various lives, common to home and college alike. The third phase was the most frustrating. Packing up to go home only to find the borders closing, having to stay back as she watched her friends leave, and then readjusting to Dubai when the repatriation eventually unsettled her again.

Anoushka is evolving as this journey progresses. She defines herself more keenly, knows her triggers and isn't quite so hard on herself. She journals, meditates and connects. 'One of my major mistakes growing up, I realize, was thinking that the adults have their stuff together. And so we work harder to prove that we have it together too if we are to be seen as adults.'

A mantra that has helped her cope is the saying 'this too shall pass'. 'When change happens anxiety hits really hard, but when you realize that you are putting yourself through long-term pain for a temporary spiral, you are able to let it go. Half your mind is telling your body to curl up in a ball, and it's a process to counter it,' she says. Her father's advice – that if she's been through so much change, there's nothing she can't cope with going forward – helps remind her she can deal with whatever changes come her way. She also reprioritizes what matters and says, 'There was a time when the only thing that mattered was grades. Now, I place the emphasis on the here and now because that's what we understand and lack a grasp on.'

Change is an infinite cycle of destruction. All things that are born begin to die. As we exit from the womb, the tree from the seed, the raindrop from the cloud, the thought from the word, an action from its cause, we are all hurtling towards an end. We do so in a similar fashion, none of us spectacularly different from each other in our creation, transformation and imminent destruction.

Change is not the exception.

We are more accustomed to change than we realize. We change every moment of our lives. We just tell ourselves that we are resistant to change because we become accustomed to the illusion of not changing. We believe that if we keep our landscape – jobs, people, homes and towns – fixed for as long as we are able to, we will not be affected by this suffering of change. While our minds may have forgotten, our spirits bear the imprints of our primordial transformations. We have been here before, a thousand times over. As much as we are constantly being destroyed, we are also constantly being born. Our bodies give birth to new skin, new hair, new nails, new cells, new antibodies and new resilience time and time again within a single lifetime. We are physically not the same person at death that we were at birth. Our thoughts replace themselves cyclically as we learn and grow. We replace old imprints, images and ideas with new ones. As educational theorist David Kolb found in 1974, we experience, reflect, conceptualize and experiment with what we know to create new learning. We learn through conditioning and observation, assimilating and accommodating, diverging and converging, and develop our own methodologies of learning unique to ourselves through our lifetime. We grey and wrinkle, we shrivel up or elongate, we become coarser or smoother, we refine and polish, we lose weight, ideas, notions, thoughts, and memories. In mind and body, we are constantly hitting refresh, consciously or not. In habit and custom, however, we have been teaching ourselves to seek comfort in repetition.

Change consumes our energy and attention. And we are primed by evolution to conserve energy. Our body uses anxiety to protect us from the danger of change. We physically tense up, we slow down, we become mentally prepared for the challenge. We save for the winters, for the impending season of lack.

In foraging and harvesting mode, when we lived off the land, we knew its mutable seasons intimately. We moved to cycles of sowing, reaping and harvesting. In the fallow months when there is no yield, we lived off what was available and conserved for when it wouldn't be. Modern cycles of living have turned our kitchens into stockpiles of preserved foods even if the market down the road provides us with off-season fruit throughout the year. As our kitchens, so our bodies and minds.

We have gone from a culture of harvesting to a culture of hoarding. We now synchronise to the seasonality of our pay cheques. As our bank balance diminishes through the month we perceive ourselves as entering a season of lack. Then, the next pay cheque comes around like rain to replenish us again. This is our freeze and thaw. Our year begins and ends with the financial one. We count our lean periods as economic, not elemental. We may have crop in the field, abundant rain, encouraging sunshine and access to nutrition, but if we are unable to acquire a specific consumer product we still count ourselves as lacking. Hence, we begin to operate in a mode of heightened conservation. The cycles of demand and supply that rule the market ensure that there is always a bit of a lack. The survival of the modern marketplace depends on it. Hence, we live in a constant state of anxiety.

Developmental psychologist Jean Piaget's Theory of Conservation measures when we gain our ability to know what stays constant when other aspects change. He found that children between ages two and four are unable to conserve because they focus on the static characteristics of objects. The ability to take in the dynamic characteristics develops later, from ages seven to eleven. Simply put, small children look at a tall glass of milk and don't understand that it's the same amount as in a short wide glass, but older children do. Conservation is a factor of logical reasoning that allows us to think in reverse, make connections and quantify what we have against what we need. This is why small children will cry if it looks like their older sibling got more. They feel deprived of their due and want things to look exactly the same.

Transfer this principle to how we eat. When we meet our personal needs by the intrinsic value of what we consume, we make healthy eating choices. We do this by choosing the amount of energy we get from units of food. When we are not able to make this logical evaluation, when we look at the static unit alone, i.e. quantity, we consume too much. We think we have less than we need or were promised, hence we want more.

A healthy eater, for instance, may know half an avocado provides the same energy as a huge breakfast of eggs with bacon and toast. Such a person is able to make the replacement by counting energy instead of units. They replace potato chips with kale, ice-cream with frozen yoghurt, candy with nuts and soda with water. If one ate the same quantity of avocados as eggs and bacon and toast, one would end up gaining weight.

Collectively, we now operate on a quantitative economic cycle, and we are losing our ability to conserve in terms of the natural cycle. The units of the former are currencies and assets. The units of the latter are nutrition, health, wellbeing.

We measure our lives in terms of the former instead of the latter. We look to quantity instead of value. Therefore, we are unable to tell when we have as much as we need. In the natural cycle, the season of lack comes annually in winter, the rest are sowing or reaping seasons. Because the economic cycle pays out weekly, monthly and annually, the lean seasons also come as frequently. We sense constant lack.

Our anxiety in the market economy is always primed. Within it, no matter how much we conserve, we will never have enough. In fact the more we hold on to common assets, the less valuable what we hold will be. The more people have access to gold deposits, the less valuable gold will be. The more people hoard currency, the less valuable the rate of exchange. The more people who are qualified for jobs, the less those jobs will pay us. It is a system that is geared against equality. The only equality in the market economy is when all of us have nothing. In owning nothing universally, we will come to equilibrium. This is why minimalism is a culture of relief from the rat race.

Equilibrium is established in nothingness.

What is nothing? As my teacher puts it, if you think nothing means nothing, try leaving all the zeroes out of your pay cheque. Zeroes have a value. Absence has value. Nothing has value.

Energy in the world is harmonized and equanimous. There is nothing to demand and nothing to give because all energy turns to matter and all matter returns to energy. A plant that absorbs sunlight and water and converts it to a new leaf is putting this principle into practice. When undisrupted, the season of lack is balanced out by the season of harvest, and the dry months by the monsoon. Some conservation is sufficient, but frenetic hoarding is unnecessary. The world flows to this seasonal rhythm from birth to death.

All we need to do is step back from the economic cycle and into the flow of the natural cycle. We recalibrate the rhythm by which we create, transform and destroy. The farmer knows all his stock will return to the earth by the next spring and will not weep over it. Tell a storekeeper he will lose all his stock in a year and he can keep only seed money, and he will be distraught. One system relies on constant renewal. The other, on artificially creating an illusion of permanence out of the essentially impermanent. From one to the other, we go from chasing the moving goalpost endlessly to an equilibrium of nothingness.

Sunyata, Nothingness, is the lack of inherent essence. There is no innate structure to anything, and therefore, there is nothing *to* last. There is only a continual and unending Anitya, Impermanence.

Changes are the material transactions by which the rapid replacement of one reality with another takes place, in the way that the seed is replaced by the birth of the shoot. Each change destroys its previous reality to be born.

Permanence simply does not exist. All capitalism can do is create the illusion of permanence. It creates this illusion through crafting a continuum, which uses the idea of legacy, of passing down, of replacing and preserving to make onlookers and participants believe there is an unbroken line of succession. A billion-dollar beauty industry stands on the illusion of preservation when cell by cell, we are every day altered. The same goes with fitness, food, homes and land, children, monuments and institutions – instruments by which we hope to fix constancy. Everything around us and in us is in a constant state of change. And all our resistance to the change is delusion.

This dissonance is the nature and the cause of our suffering.

When we recalibrate to the rhythm of the world, we seamlessly integrate our internal energy with the primordial *prana* and *qi* of the earth, and the resistance drops away. We move with the flow of change.

When the Buddha witnessed Anitya, Impermanence, he witnessed it tangibly, not as an abstract theory. He saw the *kalapas* in his own body and in all occurring phenomena in the world, microscopic particles that were constantly being replaced at such high speed they produced the illusion of permanence. The technique he used to witness this was Vipassana, right perspective. What he saw was his liberation. He realised it to be a fundamental truth of life. And that not knowing this was a cause of our suffering.

To witness Anitya is not merely a self-help tool to help you navigate the vicissitudes of life, it is the Buddha's pathway to enlightenment. Navigating change is like trekking through the wilderness and watching bridges across canyons that we just crossed collapse behind us. We may stop to look back, but we would be turned to salt trying to save it; there is nothing to be saved there. Those of us who move with our eyes on the past end up transfixed by it.

There is only one way to go and that is forward. No matter how often and how sudden the change, how large or how small, we are thrust forward through it. We are, in short spans of time and with the smallest of changes, completely transformed.

We witness people freeze in place around us every day. Those engrossed in a landscape they cannot retrace and attached to outcomes they should be releasing suffer deeply. A couple that swore to each other to prioritize family might become unhappy because one of them got a job offer they don't want to turn down. In practical everyday matters, the shifting goalpost feels like a betrayal. We build our homes on the promise of unchanging foundations, forgetting that even people held to the seeming permanence of our family structures evolve, our needs grow, and our ambitions, hopes and dreams change. Our relationship fantasies hinge on finding the eternal, the everlasting, a myth of the marriage factory. Forging a marriage for the long term is a series of everyday commitments, not one wedding bash that holds a couple together for eternity. We have to allow people their changes, as we allow ourselves our own. If we become attached to the ideal of the unchanging, we do not evolve alongside those we hold to our promise of forever. We risk getting stuck in someone else's past, who they were once to us, while they move ahead.

When we allow a moment of our own or someone else's past to define our present, we give it more value than it has earned. We keep alive the anguish of the moment in which it occurred, but also grant it the charge of the years that have passed since then. When we embrace change early on, we resolve those feelings of hurt and betrayal, see situations as worthy of release and avoid allowing them to consume so much of the energy we could have invested in other relationships in the interim.

People who plunge their attention into a specific outcome but find no surety left, move forward in a daze. We enter into new relationships without resolving the past ones. Some part of our minds and emotions remain stuck, and hold us back by surfacing when we least want them to. Someone cheated on us, and while we find love again, we begin to self-sabotage by the insecurity we have failed to release. Our minds tend to cling to the last stable place they knew, and remain there, looking back while we move forward.

Roopa Patel had been a housewife all her life until her entrepreneur husband was forced to wind up his company. With the loss of income, their family fortunes plummeted into crippling debt, he lost his confidence and was unable to start work again. She remained suspended in her glorious past for decades. Where she once hosted large community events, she was now the 'charity case', selling her gold and offering tuitions to support her family. Even when the family bungalow had to be sold and they moved into a one-room tenement, she retained the large double-door fridges that occupied too much space in her already-cramped kitchen.

She has not been able to cope with her present reality. She still cooks in the same large quantities that she used to make for guests who do not come over any more, depleting her precious food reserves faster than necessary. She spends too much on groceries, buying expensive brands and turning her nose up at cheaper options. Despite multiple arguments, she simply cannot let these habits go. They signify to her a memory of who she used to be and how she would nurture her family. In holding on to these actions she retains her hope of regaining that former social status. To surrender and adapt would mean admitting the loss of an old identity and the need to accept a new one.

We have the choice to view onward motion as destroying a lifetime's effort and a waste of our energies. Or we could embrace it as necessary, good even, and often the only way to replace corrupt and weak structures, as with outgoing governments. When we have invested time and effort in creating, it feels a waste when we have nothing to show for it. However, even discarded effort builds up to what comes next. British diver John Volanthen, who led the Tham Luang Cave rescue effort in Thailand in 2018, said after the mission, 'The last two weeks were what I had prepared for all my life.' Abdullah Abdul-Gawad was the operator of the excavator that dug the ship Ever Given out of the Suez canal in 2021. When the ship had gotten stuck, he thought it meant he would have no work that day. And while the world was making memes, he had to work alone because the other excavator operators were too scared the ship would topple on them. Life calls us up unexpectedly, and the skills that we didn't think much of in our past, the acts of banal tedium, become what have prepared us for the challenge that lies ahead.

We've all been there, wondering if there's even a point to what we do. When we see the purpose behind it, the big change that makes it all make sense, we begin to understand that what we went through reluctantly was desirable, in fact, it made us what we are. But until the change makes that purpose plain and we receive some acknowledgement, or see some tangible results of our past efforts, we remain unfulfilled. Some of us remain stuck in limbo, waiting for validation that never comes.

Rationalization about change, the conviction that everything that happened before led up to this, only works in hindsight from a position of comparative advantage. When we have achieved something lasting, all change that came before it looks good. When we are going through the change, however, there is no guarantee of the outcome. When the change seems without fruit, not giving us something better than or offering some meaning to that which preceded it, it becomes unbearable to accept.

Will we all get our win in the end? Does every gymnast who spends ten years falling off a gym horse become Nadia Comaneci? Will we, like the diver and the excavator operator, take to the media limelight and heroically rescue others and, in the process, ourselves? Will Tom Hanks play us in the movie version? If not, what was the point of all our now wasted effort?

Experience shows us we often have to tweak our expectations. We take a pay cut to work with the company of our dreams, maybe take on a lesser role, be just the deputy, we may not win a marathon but take cheer in participating. Compromise is written somewhere in the fine print, we learn quickly. It feels like a poor bargain. There is no guarantee change still won't hit us where it hurts. This leads to regrets and self-blame. If only we had made other turns, other decisions, perhaps we would have led other lives. It is burdensome to live like this, hunched over self-protectively, defensive behind our barriers, regretful, paranoid against anything that destabilises us.

When we feel attacked by change, we live fearfully. We take on the posture of a person who expects to be betrayed at every step, knocked over and blown down. We live with a fear of being cut short, undervalued and held back from reaching the full potential of our talent and skill. We doubt if we will be able to build something of equal or greater value again. We carry the burden of an imposter syndrome, doubting that we deserve what we built the first time around; that any success we have tasted came as a combination of luck, fluke or fate, and it may not in fact be replicable, for the stars may not align in the same way again. When change is the enemy, we go through life without confidence.

To live fully, openly and purposefully, therefore, we need to embrace change. To do so is not merely a Darwinian survival instinct, it is to live a life of trust. We should be able to trust in our ability to discover and attract opportunity, in our capacity to build again, be resourceful, collaborate and create. We express innate skill and talent in a way that is aligned to our sense of purpose. We find an identity that is not dependent on the support it gets and remains confident in various environments. We confront risks and falls with the bouncebackability to stand right back up again. We find the freedom to prioritize life's needs according to what matters rather than what cannot be lost.

When we live defensively, our trust is never intrinsic to us, it exists so long as external factors favour it. We create so long as the environment is supportive. We cease when these are withdrawn or altered. We are buffeted by factors we do not control. We judge our failure and success on our ability to meet specific goals. If we didn't set goals, how would we distinguish our success from our failures? And we fear failure. The function of a goal is not to be met but to validate our lives as successful. This is why we fear not meeting a goal.

In embracing change, there is no such thing as failure. In fact there are no concrete goals at all. There are multiple efforts. There are unknown paths and there is exploration of life. Our antipathy to rambling comes from the virtue we make of discipline and rigour; our timetables, schedules, curfews, the certainty of routine, our days dictated by alarms. We romanticize discipline because it is an essential unit of the market economy. Timed shifts determine pay cheques as do hours put in towards obtaining degrees and certifications. When we are rendered anxious by it all, we turn to the expansive undefined space of a vacation, or 'time off', so that we can heal and return to the elemental being.

The trick lies in moving from being a unit of market discipline to one who wields change masterfully in defiance of it.

Niranjan Iyengar, 51, an award-winning lyricist, composer and screenwriter of films such as Kal Ho Naa Ho, *underwent a process of voluntary change after his mother's passing, that saw him questioning his conservative values, disciplined practices and sense of rigour. These are his lessons from it:*

'Change is something that is frightening. It's terrifying on many levels, but it is also something that is so inspiring if you manage to hit the right note. Ultimately, knowing the song and singing the song are two different things. So what happens is you keep trying to sing, you keep trying to sing, you keep trying to sing, and some day you hit the right note. And that's what happens with change.

'My friend Srishti Arya said something that stayed with me: "This is a journey you have to go on. Either you go laughing, singing or you are pulled by your hair kicking and screaming." I am always kicking and screaming. In retrospect it seems like that. I am currently in the process of drastic change. My discomfort with change has been evident to me from 2014. While I had begun to feel the restlessness, when one is as resistant to change as I am, we miss the tell-tale signs that it is coming. We ignore it because we don't want to face change. Because the moment you accept the change you have to realign certain things in your life which you are probably comfortable with. Any change causes discomfort. It's a comfort with the status quo. Most of us are very good with others' change but terrible with our own. When you are in a positive space and want to make a change, that change is easy. It's when you are in a negative space and you know deep down something is wrong, that's when it is hard to make a change. The mind is like the body.

Just before you get a cold, you will have an irritation in the throat. When you ignore it, you will reach a cold and when you ignore the cold you will reach the fever. If you ignore the fever it reaches something else. Change is like this. It sends us the warning signs but we ignore it. Whatever we ignore sits in the body. The body wears the trauma of the change you're ignoring.

'I have always avoided change. I love the status quo since childhood. My relationships have been extremely strong. This comes from saying that once I have committed to this, this will not change. There is no good thing or bad thing about it, it is how change works for you. Change is always inevitable. While cerebrally, through knowledge, books and people, you know this to be the truth, there is a difference between knowing the song and singing it. To sing it you have to practise. I have been feeling there is something that needs to change in me for a very long time. All through my twenties and thirties, I was the person living "the correct way to live". If it is not enforced, it's okay. I was not hiding, pretending. I met a lot of people like Pooja Bhatt, Manish Malhotra, Karan Johar, Srishti Arya, Ryan Stephen, who wanted me to lighten up a bit and I was constantly surrounded by people and their joie de vivre. But they were also drawn to my core of rigour and discipline because they are all also hard-working people. When you change, you lose only those people who are not aligned to you at a core level and you've only connected with superficially. When you change your script, if your core is aligned, those people withstand your change.

'Change is very important. It is something your insides are telling you to do. There is a core that does not change, that you hold on to, and that has a commonality with the genuine connections around you. As you are changing, the people around you are changing too. After every change there is a breather. As others change you take a breather, as you change others take a breather, but there is a collective movement forward. There have been movements of their change that have been uncomfortable for me, and change that I go through that is uncomfortable for them. Srishti and I used

to speak twice a day. Now we speak once in two months. But when you know the core is strong, then the dynamic and friendship doesn't change. I feel everybody aligns to the change that you go through.

'People say when you accept change you enjoy that growth. I know in my head I am not comfortable with change. It is never pleasant. It's like a workout. They keep telling you that you will get used to it, but honestly I never do. To me the aspect of change that helps me is that there are times you do things out of the excitement of it. And when the excitement wanes it will have affected the change that is required. I give myself a deadline and dedicate myself to a change until the deadline and will hope the time will be sufficient to meet a goal. I need to find some level of excitement for the change. By the time the excitement dies down the change will already have been effected.

'I began learning Hindustani classical music at the age of 32. I used discipline to move past the inertia, by which time the change had set in. A negative change will push you surely and steadily towards a positivity depending on how it plays out in your life. From 31 to now at 50, I've been changing what was once a particularly disciplined rhythm of my life and I know now that no change is entirely negative or positive in itself. It's how you use the change to propel you forward.'

The happy-go-lucky Fool of the Tarot, a meagre bundle of essentials on a stick thrown over the shoulder, makes his journey with his skill in his hands, trust in his heart and hope in his mind. He sets forth on a journey into the unknown, leaping lightly over treacherous crevices, foraging for the day and trusting his tomorrows to tomorrow. He moves with confidence because whatever comes, he trusts himself to navigate it.

Anitya, Impermanence is the essence of life, and those of us who are able to embrace it, navigate it.

2

How to Be a Mountain

AT THE START OF THE TWENTIETH CENTURY THERE WAS neither running water nor electricity available across the world, while the start of the twenty-first assumes equal access to technology is a right. Both centuries have catalogued the most rapid change among humankind since a meteor wiped out the dinosaurs. Yet, we still speak of transformation as that which applies to species and technological advances other than ourselves, contemplating it in third person, studying it through microscopes and academic papers from a safe distance. We are strangely specific about whom change should impact for it to be good. Disruption is a great buzzword for technology and start-ups, as long as its founders are stable. When confronted by change ourselves, we are resistant and unwilling to adapt.

This is because change is conditionally desirable only when it is within our control. We want change that is predictable and purposeful, like a planned implosion to bring an abandoned building down. Change that does not fit these parameters takes away our sense of being able to manage it. It makes light of our master plan. We need to decide when change occurs, how it occurs, and whom it impacts. Then, under these circumstances, we view change as good.

Stability is not just virtue, it is reiterated; it is the source of our peace. When the pursuit of this stability becomes too much for us, when we feel it slipping away or becoming too all-consuming, we seek refuge in it externally, in the mountains. They impact us for so many reasons, their seemingly effortless permanence being one.

With their moody, changing weather the mountains are whom we run to when we seek to heal from the demanding-ness of our lives. They stand a paradox of permanence, reminding us of what stays when nothing else does. In being so, they allow us our dichotomies, the desire for mutable days around the appearance of a stable core. Because we forget that the mountains are constantly transforming too. They undergo a more glacial pace of change that makes it less perceptible to us. The mountains are so imposing they distract us from contemplating the sea beds they no longer nurture. They absorb their pasts and futures into their present. In their now, so are we in ours.

This makes the mountains undemanding companions, accepting our imperfections, of thick socks, moth-eaten jumpers, comfortable shoes and mismatched layers as we huff up inclines, immersed in self-absorption. On a misty walk, we may nod to passers-by and pull into a by-lane of solitude. Serenaded by an orchestra of squirrels and a sonata of birds, a breeze scented by pines and eucalyptus, we inhale it deeply in a moment that is urgently attention-seeking. That gasp in our chest is awe and fullness. The instant is perfect, and we are both made whole in each other's presence.

A serenity spreads over everything in the presence of something not merely greater than ourselves, but in greater command of itself than we are. The mountain has seen a millennia of change, and our grappling with our decades seems so insignificant by comparison. This is what makes it possible to surrender to the moment. In the radiating calm, we find ourselves at peace. We find a harmony with the energy of the natural universe.

We come to stillness.

Robert Pirsig in *Zen and the Art of Motorcycle Maintenance* said the only Zen you find at the top of the mountain is the Zen you bring there. Osho asked us to consider the opposite – that the peace of the mountain is actually the peace you leave up there.

For most of us moving to the rhythm of an economic cycle, such a core of calm is hard to sustain. Few of us have the luxury of escaping to our idyllic corners, waiting for epiphanies to arrive. I mean there are flights to catch, hotels to book, leaves of absence to be sanctioned, plants to be watered, dogs to be walked and fed, milk subscriptions to be cancelled and co-ordinations of all kinds from the weather to the mood to take into account. So if you're lucky, you have had one of these. Once. Some time ago. You remember. You think. Oh wait, no, you're thinking of the wallpaper you briefly had on your desktop in 2012. So we depend on the factors that contribute to it. We depend on the beauty of our environment, meditative music, money, friendships, the success of our ventures, the accessibility of our goals, the validation of our peers, none of which we actually control.

We piece our peace from the fragments of our lives.

However, stillness is not a peace that comes and goes. Stillness remains, whether the mountain remains a mountain or a seabed. It is what stays with you regardless of the time that has passed, the environment, what you bring to your success or to your peers and loved ones. **You are your own mountain.**

Stillness is both an instrument and an outcome.

It is the quiet that occurs when the clamour in your mind and body has ceased. The clamour ceases when you shift out of a posture of defensiveness and fear. You shift your posture when you no longer feel attacked by change, circumstances, external factors, other people or your thoughts. When you no longer feel attacked, you're not in a defensive mode. When you're not in a defensive mode, you're not reactive. When you're not reactive, you begin responding to your environment. Responsiveness makes collaboration, friendship and pooling of resources possible. When you collaborate you feel interconnected with others. The interconnection puts you at ease, in collaboration with the forces of life, not in opposition to them. When your relationships are no longer oppositional, your goals feel more accessible. Because now your goals are not in competition with others' goals. When they are not in competition, they become less rigid. If not this, another, and so in their dynamism and flexibility, they become accessible. When you are able to set accessible goals, you're able to set boundaries against what doesn't contribute to your meeting them. When you set boundaries, you take charge of your life. When you take charge of your life, you cease to be a victim. When you cease to be a victim, you're no longer a puppet, you become the puppeteer. When you're the puppeteer, you gain power. When you gain power in this way, it is rooted within. When it is rooted within, it is no longer subject to being buffeted by external factors. When it is no longer buffeted, you operate in stillness, and what clouds may obscure your sky on occasion, in fact, add to the scenic beauty of your path.

How to be your own mountain:

The Taoist practice of qigong meets yoga where the Chinese mountain pose meets tadasana or samasthiti. Both cultivate the harmony of life energy, or prana, *in the physical body. Stand upright, feet aligned with the shoulders and flat on the floor. Your toes should point forwards, with your arms loosely by the sides of the body, but held slightly apart from the torso, palms facing outwards. Relax your shoulders such that they are not hunched up but aligned and thrown back, which will nudge your spine straight. This should lift your chest without puffing it up. Dip your chin slightly such that your gaze is parallel to the ground.*

The qigong version takes the legs wider and keeps the knees soft. Yoga focuses on prana, which takes an upward movement. Qigong focuses on earthing through the feet, the downward movement. You can assume whichever posture you prefer.

When you assume this posture, you should feel a sense of expansion and openness through your body. Stay in posture, avoid tilting to one side or the other and remain centred.

Breathe naturally, observing your breath rising and falling. Be aware of the flow of air and the sensations in your body. Draw your focus inward to the mind, the body, the flow of air and energy, your natural breathing patterns and the sensations on your body. Consider the qualities of a mountain and what it must feel to be one. Feel fixed, rooted, steadfast, energized, balanced and able to withstand what comes at you. You should feel a harmonious alignment between your thoughts, body and energy.

Hold the pose for anywhere from a minute to ten minutes.

3

The Master and the Monk

The master was getting old.
His eyesight and hearing were failing.
He summoned the apprentice monk and said,
'I have taught you all I can teach you. You are now free to go.'
The monk did not leave.
The master's voice began to break, and so he wrote on a piece of paper,
'I have taught you all I can teach you. You are now free to go.'
The monk did not leave.
As he lay dying, the master summoned the monk to his side
and whispered with his dying breath,
'I have taught you all I can teach you. You are now free to go.'
The monk replied,
'Master, it is you who are leaving, not me.
You are now free to go.'
The master died, at peace, that night.
The monk became the master.

~

IT FEELS LIKE A TALL ORDER TO STAND AMID WHAT IS FALLING apart and envision the possibilities. How do we know that we aren't being naively-optimistic, toxically positive, and unseeing of the chaos? During the pandemic, from India to Brazil, we've seen the avoidable loss caused by governments that insist things are fine, or going to be fine, and refuse to prepare for the fallout. We need to act when it is timely, and need to have systems that will man the lifeboats rather than play the cellos while the Titanic sinks. What distinguishes the master enthralled by his own leadership from the sanguine baton-taking of the monk?

The difference is nostalgia for the past in contrast with the reality of the present. The ability to see reality as it is, not as one wants it to be, is what the Buddha called 'Yathā bhūta ñāna dassana' (the knowledge and vision according to reality).

When we are open to influences and opportunities, we are expansive, taking chances that connect us, and become able to form collaborations for the future. When we are insular, closed to and suspicious of that which seeks to impact us, we become restricted and diminished by our change. The first allows us to flow in a continuum, the other stalls us, grasping at permanence.

The monk doesn't become a master because he inherits a titular position, he becomes one because he steps into this continuum. Because he sees the value of a knowledge cycle that is larger than himself. He bears witness to the fading in and out of monks and masters. He too will be replaced when his time comes, hopefully by a young monk with a vision that takes his own further. Unlike the artificial perpetuity of the market economy, the monk rests in the knowledge that he is imminently replaceable. He is not pursuing the illusion of his permanence. He owns no legacy. He dwells in the compassion that comes from recognizing the frailty of human attachment, its urge to bequest and endow, and the starkness of his detachment in contrast to it.

How does a monk inherit the role of the master? The monk is able to take a legacy forward because he retains the essence of the master within him.

Is a mountain the rock, the shape, the height, the placement among a range of mountains, is it its snow, forests, wildlife? What is its 'mountain-ness'? Is it only a mountain because all of us have agreed to call it a mountain? A mountain in this way both exists and does not. This is what is meant by absence of inherent essence. There is nothing within it that is definitively a mountain. The awareness of this on a much vaster scale is Sunyata, Nothingness. Since things do not have inherent essence, there is nothing to pass down, which also means there is nothing lost.

The mountain does not become less of a mountain when it is grated down to sand, in its elemental form. In fact, it is now able to mutate into so much more and embrace the world in a wider way, a vase, a window pane, a brick. If it is knowledge, wisdom, practice, tradition, the seat, the teaching, the robes, the passing on of it all passes the master on. This ability to not only remain undiminished by change, but also to be made expansive by it is what makes one a master.

We are each a continuum through our lives, an accumulation of karmas and a sum of actions and reactions, causes and conditions, and our struggles to overcome them. Hence, true mastery is never just momentary, or a phase of success, or when a man is briefly feted. The race isn't to be on the cover of *Forbes* this year, but to make progress such that one doesn't carry the burden of the past nor return to lessons left unlearned. A surefooted progress keeps one at peace, harmony and integrated with other beings. The monk is playing the long game towards mastery, across many lives, and is conserving his energy for the marathon. He who chases a fleeting success is making a sprint to the first visible mountain and imagines there are no other ridges to conquer and no more landscape to gain.

The accommodative perspective, one that is inclusive of the shifting goalpost and the expanding landscape, is what allows us to navigate Dukkha, dissatisfaction and the suffering of change. We are neither elated by significant achievement nor put down by the lack of it, because our perspective looks beyond one's limited self. Take, for example, the monolith of the Kailasa temple or the caves of Ajanta and Ellora. These were crafted by a series of ascetic and monk sculptors over a couple of centuries, beginning somewhere around 735–756 CE and carried out through the reigns of various kings, each with their unique religious proclivities. If they were monuments raised by a single master artist, they could not have been so painstakingly crafted; one lifetime would simply not have been enough. Equally, if the original vision, the knowledge and skill to execute it had not been shared through a sense of legacy and interconnection, the final structure would not have been so cohesive. To be masters, we must feel this kinship in our core. Our legacies must flow beyond the scopes of our bodies and our lives, the limits of who gets the credit for it. And this kinship necessarily is what tides us over change, the knowledge that we do not end here and neither does our work.

Within our more finite idea of mastery, we think of it like taking university classes, getting a degree and achieving accolades for what we have learned. We are now 'masters' of the arts and sciences. We are there. We have arrived. We expect acknowledgement for our mastery because we have 'completed' a course of study. We assume this arrival marks the end of a struggle, a completion of what we have worked towards.

Except, it doesn't.

Mastery is that which exponentially increases the struggle. It now amplifies it on behalf of everybody else involved. This is why true masters work tirelessly.

Mastery is an incessant run on the hamster wheel. Those who have created a beast constantly engaged in creation – of ideas, a product, an art form and their by-products of wealth, success and fame – have to constantly feed the beast or it will consume them. This could be a skill, an image or a company. You breed an imposter syndrome for knowing too less, doing too little. When you become too big to fail, you are called upon to innovate. The definition of success, lo and behold, changes. It becomes, surprise surprise, a shifting goalpost. Success must beget more success or else it is now a failure. You now have family, employees, followers and stakeholders of various kinds who depend on you to keep doing what you are doing. You become the progenitor of future stability. You are responsible for the endurance of your input but also of your output, a legacy plan, the effluents of your trade, the far-reaching social impact, environmental sustainability and the microcosmic behaviours you allow to replicate, calibrating and sharing your privilege.

Mastery is to become a creator consumed by their creation. When the violin becomes the Stradivarius. When the 'bindu' becomes S.H. Raza. When the monk becomes the master. When the creator and the creation are one, only one of them remains. When the creation assumes the identity of the previous reality and eliminates it, then mastery is achieved.

For such merging, surrender is essential. You have to be willing to be eliminated.

Surrender of the individual in the wake of the multitude, surrender of the primary vision to the legacy, surrender of the attachment to the outcome, surrender of the immediate successes for the long game, surrender of finality of supremacy to the work that doesn't end.

We seek the title of master, which we hope to gain with the rigour of the monk, but we seek it without his propensity for surrender. **The first act of the monk is surrender.**

The mountain may stand for a thousand years, but if it is to survive, and be more than a lump of rock quickly eroded down to the elements that comprise it, it must offer the refuge of its body. To seeds and saplings born by the wind and bird droppings, it must host forests, and within them diverse wildlife, from leopards and deer to squirrels, monkeys and rodents. It must lend its face generously to weather storms filled with raging wind, lashing rain and striking lightning. Because in as much as the mountain hosts them, inanimate as he is, unmoving, they nurture and shape him, and he lives on in them, shaping their trajectories as much as they shape his. To be a mountain is much more than being simply large or unmissable. It is being scalable, replicable, steal-able, ownable. To be a mountain is to belong incessantly.

We often attempt to own the mountain. It is easier than being one. It requires less self-involvement, self-surrender. All we need is money and all money needs is hard work, everything else remaining constant. But everything else doesn't remain constant. And thus, those who seek to own the mountain will soon be owned by it.

A line of Rumi's poetry from book one of *Masnavi* goes:

> *...very little grows on jagged rock. Be ground.*
> *Be crumbled, so wildflowers will come up where you are.*

This is the only way to not be defined by the cycles of failure and success, to be constantly participating in and contributing to the change that comes our way. We have to own the change, we have to be the change, we have to contribute to the change, taking a participative role rather than a victim role. Our bodies and minds must become that from which the change arises.

The man whose stability is kept intact by things around him remaining stable, in times of environmental instability acts out of fear. An inability to control factors external to himself leaves him angry and frustrated. A koan tells the following story: Ryokan Taigu, a Zen master, was sitting outside his hut contemplating the moon when a thief came by and stealthily robbed his meagre possessions. As he was leaving, Ryokan beckoned him and gave him the clothes he was wearing. As the bewildered thief left, Ryokan glanced at the moon and said, 'I wish I could have given him this moon as well.'

The paradox of monkhood, rigorous discipline that does *not* result in material success, seems like a cruel joke. We are always chasing the 'secrets' of the monks, how to manifest, how to let go, mindfulness, but we don't truly want to adopt their ways. Why do the men with the least use for worldly insight, discipline and knowledge seem to have an abundance of it? Well, one reason is that true masters are not reactive but responsive. So they may not seem to participate in the race for transitory gain.

They are not springing at every opportunity that comes their way, they are waiting to gain ground in what they value. They are abundant, but they pursue a different kind of abundance. We only view the form that is apparent and valuable to us.

We reject the idea of monkhood because it seems tedious, onerous and a form of self-deprivation. Who hurt you enough to want to be a monk, we think. We imagine it to be a process of exclusion. We fear that we must set aside our family and friends, and give up the habits and routines we enjoy, our carefully cultivated tastes, belongings, all acts of creation and self-expression and live sparsely. This seems like a giving up. We are a 'live well' generation. What is the point of living if not to amass? And what is the point of amassing if we cannot enjoy life and share it with those we love? How do we share if in order to accumulate we must surrender? Nothing about this equation seems to add up.

The monk becomes a master through his surrender, and he practises this surrender in his meditations. We commonly conceive of meditation as a concerted effort towards exclusion. We imagine surrendering as a state of sitting quiet, controlling our thoughts and feeling peaceful but getting nothing done. We add these to the list of things we need to feel and do, and it becomes another chore. We have to shut out our distractions. When in fact this is what meditation is not. We don't stop hearing the things around us or feeling our sensory inputs. We don't stop belonging to the society we are a part of and the systems we are born into. Meditation does not and cannot begin with the negative. People who are constantly trying not to think, hear, feel or be distracted are not meditating. They are struggling in vain against themselves and their interconnection with the world around them. This is the antithesis of meditation.

We begin to meditate when we simply observe our environment as well as our role as its observer. Meditation begins with acceptance – of sounds, sensations, thoughts, feelings, everything. This is a process of inclusion; done right, it should lead us to bear witness to our interconnection. We witness the impact a sensory input has on us, whether it's food, a word, a memory or a mosquito bite. We witness our reaction in thought, word, sensation and action, and how that translates into what we put out into the world. We observe the reaction that it causes in turn. When we make the connections between this ripple effect of action and reaction, we see that nothing, no event or deed, no person, neither us nor them, acts or exists in isolation. Then, as we sit in contemplation, we begin to open the doors to the world around us, seeing them truly as extensions of ourselves. We begin to see things as they really are.

The monk does not reject life or the world or action. He simply surrenders his attachment to his intended outcomes from it because all possible outcomes become okay. A wave is not just a part of an ocean. Each wave is elementally the ocean. What sense does it make to be angry or hurt at the rise of one or the crash of the other? There is nothing to grasp at. Our rise will come and our fall will come too. One day we will crash, another we will vaporize and return, a drop to the self-same ocean that created and destroyed us. We do what we can, but we also now act in the context of this larger cycle. Nothing we do occurs in isolation.

It is a pragmatic world view. Those who do not witness the interconnections have a hard time grasping it, because to them the world is finite, like a cake, and if you don't hurry to get your slice, it will be finished and you will be left without. The monk's point of view is that there is nothing finite about it, it is a constantly self-replenishing ocean, and so I do not gain when others lose, nor does my loss benefit another. To be part of a collective and yet be separate is not to surrender identity. It is to nurture connection in a more integrated way. This can sometimes be really hard to do in a system that values ownership over harmony.

Rajesh and Tina Agarwal began a phase of incessant quarrelling after 12 years of marriage. Their problem is a state of too much togetherness. Tina demands that they have date nights where they go out for a nice meal or watch movies together, socialize and go for walks. Rajesh has been asking his wife for some space. He'd rather read a book, work out or meet old college friends. He's always with family or at work and has very little time for the things he wants to do as an individual. Tina is annoyed that the goalpost in their marriage, which she thought was togetherness, has shifted. Annoyed, she has stopped asking her husband how he is when he comes home from work. She deliberately plans outings with her friends when he is going to be home, hoping that he will notice her absence and miss her. Instead, frustrated that she simply doesn't get him and isn't giving him the space he needs with grace, Rajesh simmers with resentment. Neither is he peaceful in the space he has, since it comes as a punishment, nor is she genuinely enjoying the activities she has planned for herself. Unable to keep pace with each other, they struggle with this equation and file for divorce a year later. They tell the court they have 'grown apart'. Each blames the other for changing.

We can give each other space because of anger, feeling rejected and taking it personally, with sullen silences that further need to be appeased. The space becomes another object of contention in an already contentious relationship. Or we can individually lead full and separate lives, with friendships, hobbies, travels and adventures that also mesh together to craft fulfilling spaces both together and apart. We can be complimentary to each other. This is also a form of togetherness. One operates from fear of loss, the other from the security of belonging. One has identity only when the union is complete, the other has an identity independent of the union and is further fulfilled by the coming together.

Rejection is a disengagement that emerges from disappointment and failure, hurt and anger. The monk is not angry at the world. He just doesn't need its constant attention to feel any more fulfilled than he already is. With mastery, the world becomes an expression of oneself. When we are happy in our own space, engaged, creative, attuned with ourselves, our partner is able to, or should ideally be able to, find joy in our joy. This oneness that comes from another's fulfilment, stems from compassion. Instead of dividing joy between two people and making it a finite object with limited capability to be shared, like, you know, a pie. When we are able to tack on the joy of several others onto one's own, we make it expansive.

Why do those who have least use for billions seem to draw it to themselves? Every person who visits it enjoys the Dalai Lama's gold-plated palace on his behalf. His sense of person has become so expansive, as wide as an ocean, that his ownership does not become selfish or limited to his physical sphere. The enjoyment of others is a part of his own. The participation of others becomes his collaboration. Their gain becomes his gain too, just like a child taking the last morsel of food from a mother's plate satiates the mother. The separateness ceases. This is the way of the bodhisattva, the being that lends his own liberation to help others find theirs.

We all know people who refuse to participate in social gatherings, competitions and events. They believe that secluding themselves from hurt protects them from the pain of loss, grief and failure. By rejecting life we think we can reject loss, but in truth, we are rejecting gain as well. Exclusion is unnatural by definition because we are products of our circumstances, a link in the chain of cause and effect and part of a whole. We are elemental to the energy of the world. So, to use rejection as a philosophy of life is to deny our true nature and wage constant battle against it. There is no stillness in that.

The true mastery of the monk is his ability to embrace both loss and gain with equanimity because the outcomes don't alter his reality.

In our everyday pursuits, we seek to embrace the gain but not the loss and end up rejecting both. To gain we have to actively engage with the loss, not just tolerate it.

Pick a side:

Imagine you have invited a couple, Mr Gain and Ms Loss, over for dinner. You love the husband – you are old friends from college. But you can't stand the wife – she has a shrill voice, dresses loudly, is intrusive and annoys you by her very existence. If you simply tolerate her, are rude to her or ask her to leave, you lose the friendship of the husband too. He is not coming back to you because they make a team; they go hand in hand and are lifelong complements to each other. If you embrace her with the warmth and hospitality you embrace him with, you will befriend both and they will both come and go from your home as old friends.

Loss and gain are two sides of a coin. You cannot seek one and shun the other. The transition between the two, the periodic flipping of the coin, is change. When we befriend both we find equanimity.

~

A master does not cease to be part of the world. He still thinks, still feels, still acts. He is not freed from having traits that are intrinsic to human nature. An ant biting a meditating monk still inflicts a pinch of pain. The monk just doesn't react to it.

To be a master is to no longer be the puppet of actions, thoughts and feelings. This does not mean he doesn't experience them, just that they don't direct his responses.

We feel a plethora of emotions that sail through our heads like monsoon clouds. We imagine the master doesn't. That he feels no anger, no sadness, no frustration, no fear, no irritation, no confusion, no sense of loss, grief or pain and also no joy, no longing, no yearning, no wanting, no craving – a life with neither lows nor highs.

Just imagine a life like that.

No, truly imagine it.

To watch your child take her first steps into school and not feel love and sadness at her growing up all at once. To lose a parent and feel no grief. To break up from a loved one and feel no anger, pain or sorrow. To look back on happy memories and feel no nostalgia. To look back on lost opportunities and feel no regret. To catch a glimpse of a loved one, a crush maybe, and feel zero longing to be with them. To feel nothing.

How can this be ideal?

Kiara is 32 and has been coping with immense fear, anger, guilt and sadness. She feels frozen after the death of a loved one in an accident that left another with a disability. She has sunk into a depression and feels the weight of the emotional changes she's going through. She feels disrupted, has lost confidence and sees her parents unable to cope with the loss. Through all the uncertainty, her single greatest gain from it, she says, has been resilience, the realization that change is life.

It is through the crucible of our emotions that we arrive at the realizations that anchor our forward progress.

Psychologically, when people feel nothing, they have repressed their emotions to such a degree that they have become numb. Victims of abuse often experience this. Some may take to self-harm or cutting themselves with superficial surface wounds or piercings to simply feel pain that conveys to them a sense of being alive, of being relevant, of existing. Pain, hurt and anger validate our experience of life as much as laughter and joy do. As Jim Morrison put it, '…pain is something to carry like a radio. You feel your strength in your experience of pain. It's all in how you carry it. That's what matters. Pain is a feeling. Your feelings are a part of you. Your own reality. If you feel ashamed of them and hide them, you're letting society destroy your reality. You should stand up for your right to feel pain.'

These emotions, all the upheaval, are what convey to us the substance of life itself. They are what shape us and our relationships with the world around. They direct our paths towards and away from events, people, places and circumstances. For those whose experience of life troubles them, self-medication through drugs and alcohol is a way of running away from feeling anything at all. This need to not feel becomes overwhelming until it begins to consume all of you – your time, energy, money, dedication and focus. When it has taken over, the self-assigned cure consumes everything like an invasive plant species in a garden that begins to block out the sun. You'll have to take the hedge scissors to it. You'll need to set aside the addiction and its associated numbness and to feel, to confront fully the unaddressed emotions. To sit on the lawn and feel the heat of everything that's beating down on you – sun, wind, rain, hail, all of it. These may be self-blame or blame on others, guilt, regret, anger, betrayal, sadness or loneliness. Whatever the emotion may be, we learn from life that we need to feel fully, deeply and freely to sustain ourselves.

So why would the ideal be to feel nothing? What is the purpose of our lives then, why are we even human if the ideal is to feel nothing? To turn ourselves to stone surely cannot be the aspiration and purpose of human birth, which we are told is rare and precious.

Having said that, we also do not want to be constantly on a Ferris wheel of emotionality, up and down, windswept by the gale of the day. We would like to be able to regulate how we feel, how much we feel, how deeply we feel and when we feel. We don't want to be crying over perceived slights, our choices dictated by harsh judgement. We want to be able to get over break-ups, broken friendships and insults and move on. As much as we do not want to be broken, dislodged or obstructed in our goals, when we are we want to be able to gather up the pieces and build a new life out of what remains. We want to be able to snap out of bleakness when we are done with self-indulgence. We want to be able to mend, heal and forge more adjustable connections that move with our own changing goals and contexts. We want flexibility to neither be stuck in a prison of our overwhelming emotions nor be completely rid of them.

This is what mastery looks like.

It is to be in charge of one's thoughts, feelings and actions, to be able to calibrate them and not live devoid of them.

Stagnancy is not stability.

Those who have mastered change are not those who never change but those who are not deterred by change.

We can spend a long time being afraid to implement changes that would lead us to new learnings. Even when we know to make them can rid us of painful pasts. We can have those rich and fulfilling life experiences we seek, if we don't mind the discomfort that comes along with it, in the way that a child that plays a great game will invariably scrape his knee, or even lose the match. Yet, we delay making these changes and mistake this for a trade-off in favour of stability.

You may be outwardly stable and inwardly in disarray. You may be outwardly in a constant state of motion and inwardly calm.

Stillness does not belong to he who does not move, but to he who moves with the natural rhythm of life.

OCEAN

Samudaya, the Pursuit of Permanence

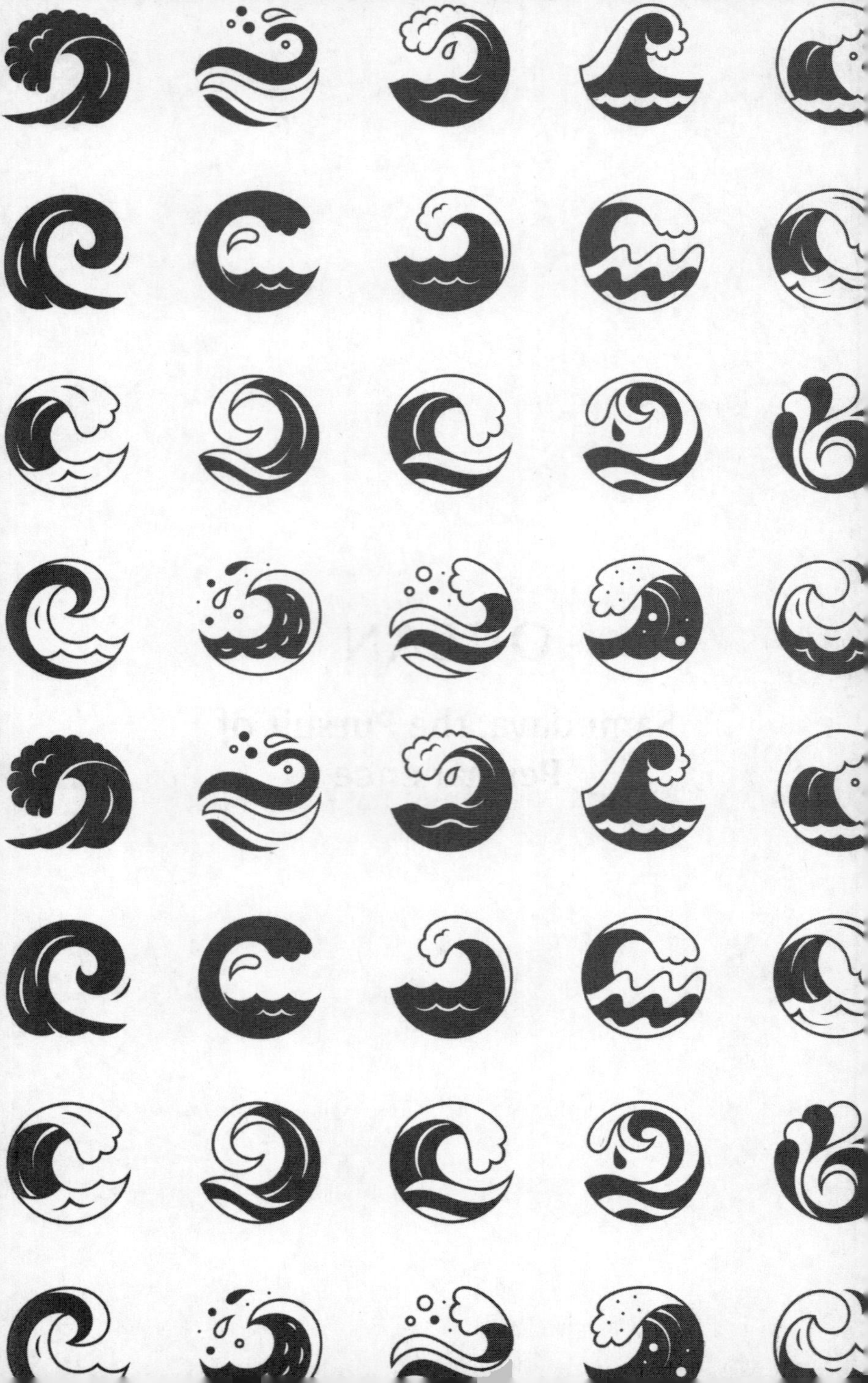

4

Object Permanence

A RESEARCH ICEBREAKER NAVIGATING THE BERG-POCKED scape of the southern Indian Ocean cuts through a floating shelf, thawing what has lain frozen for centuries. One newborn wave crashes into a myriad of blues; cerulean, azure, Nile, Oxford, peacock, periwinkle, pewter, Prussian, aquamarine, each so different from the deep dark womb of midnight she has emerged from. She gasps in the chilly air that flurries up her mane with froth and foam. Giddy with energy, she lurches this way and that. She surfs with the wind and rides the tide. She confronts angry rips and is carried along by subversive currents. She bounces off sandy shores, hitchhiking on the backs of whales and cruising on the noses of dolphins. Playful, forgetful until she looks around and realizes she has no clue which way is home again. 'I am lost,' she wails, weeping herself out in salty tears until she evanesces into vapour under the glinting Mediterranean sun. Unburdened, she rains upon herself, salt to salt, breath to breath, falling hither and thither. A cargo ship on the Dardanelles cuts through a serene glass of blue, releasing a multitude of new-born waves from their slumber.

There are three kinds of psychological uncertainties – probability, ambiguity and complexity. The first is when we don't know the outcome, the second when we don't know the risks associated with the outcome and the third is when we don't know the multiple influences and impacts affecting the outcome. There's also a distinction between ignorance and uncertainty. Sometimes we don't know because we haven't enquired or because we lack the tools of enquiry. However, sometimes no matter how much we enquire, we don't find the answers.

Whichever kind of uncertainty we may be facing, all change is intrinsically violent in nature. Change is both a cleaving from and a cleaving to, precipitated by a sudden act of dislodgement. It is a rebirthing, the coming together of particles or events forcefully enough to shift the trajectory. Be this a cloudburst that swerves a river from its course, the pressure on carbon to make a diamond, an eruption that pushes up an island where there was none before or a sexual congress that leads to a baby. All change is forceful and disruptive. Divorce is a violence, birth is a violence, relocation is a violence – each realigns us on distinct mind, body and spirit levels. When we re-engage we have to reconsider our identities; our bodies respond differently and our spiritual perspective is altered. Even the changes we see as glacial gradually reach a **tipping point**, like the rising heat of water just as it bursts into a rolling bubble. In the tipping point lies the turn we take, the expansion of form, thought and spirit, allowing ourselves to connect with another form, another path, another course of events, and be forever altered from this point onwards. Resistance rises with the simmer that hurtles towards change as we battle with our instinct to maintain the status quo.

It can seem distinct – everything that went before and everything that came after – like two parts of a broken life that can't ever connect again. However, cleave is a contranym, a word that means its opposite as well and applies equally to both, what we detach from and what we attach to. The parts are united in a continuum that can be hard to sense when in a process of alteration, like a river that runs underground for a stretch. Water transforms from gas to liquid to solid, sweat or vapour or ice many times over and yet, it remains elementally the same. It can be hard to see the correlation between a floating ice shelf in the Antarctic and the sweat on your brow. Yet, because scientists tell us so and we study the lifecycle of water in schools, we understand this link to be fact. Our personal transformations seem much more incomprehensible because we don't study them in this way. When we witness our own change, we're looking from iceberg to sweat and wondering how we got from one to the other. The in-between is lost to us and seems unbridgeable. We seem to understand transformation better when we study it in others, caterpillar to butterfly, winter to spring, but less in ourselves. All natural elements undergo such necessary transformation; we are not the exception to the rule.

Don't despair when you see that suffering is a fact. There is a cause of suffering, Samudaya. This is the Buddha's Second Noble Truth.

That there is a cause is a Truth in itself because it leads us to the insight that if something begins, it also ends. We need to know that suffering is not endless, it is also Anitya, Impermanent, and it has a source.

The pursuit of permanence is a cause of suffering. When we witness the imperative nature of change, we go from being shocked by the turn, to anticipating it. Change is not an if, it is a when. When we understand this, we can move our efforts from the act of maintaining resistance to it, which is not just futile but also exhausting, to smoothening its passage.

Such transformation comes easier to us when we witness it in our own physical and physiological changes. When we transform from childhood to puberty or from a state of singlehood to motherhood, we note the visible factors of change and put in cultural and social support systems to acclimatize. There is a ready body of advice, there are rituals and rites of passage by which to navigate these waters. We give teenagers space, boundaries and rules, we assign them autonomy, set rewards and punishments. We encourage independence and social relationships. We honour the newfound independence with gifts and responsibilities. We recognize the stage as developmentally crucial to prepare them for early adulthood. Concepts like independence, fidelity and purpose are nurtured here. Such acclimatization is essential to the growth process.

Object permanence is the theory that we trust things are there even when we can't see them. We trust in the permanence of things even when there is no evidence to it. In 1936, Piaget observed babies around eight months of age as they burst into tears when a blanket or a toy was taken away from them. Think of the times when you may have played peek-a-boo with a baby. The baby thinks you are no longer there if it can't see your face and becomes concerned. When you uncover your face, the child feels reassured. This is a lack of object permanence. It is a test of working memory. Your cognition doesn't have the capacity to grasp beyond the present moment. Once the reassurance sets in, you believe what has gone will come back, you remember what went away in the past came back and you don't panic so much. Between 18 and 24 months, the baby is able to understand that even if toys are hidden in boxes or put away, they still exist; that Mom will return even if she's gone out. A good grasp of object permanence assuages separation anxiety and eases our transitions through life. Because we know what went before will come again, that these states of transition are an inevitable part of life and that there is nothing to worry about. We trust that things we can't see support us and will be restored to us. Object permanence is not needing things around us be fixed permanently. It is trusting that we will find what we need when we need it. It is to be okay with the change of having things taken away or restored.

The ability to cope with change is to come at life from a position of trust.

After working in hospitality for 10 years, Joanna D'Souza went on maternity leave. Having children was always important to her, but she also intended to return to work to claim a promotion that she had earned. She feels lucky to have supportive in-laws who live nearby, which means ready childcare. Her anxiety is driven by the physical changes to her body. She has rapidly gained over 10 kg due to hormonal changes. She feels bloated and is unable to stand long hours, which is a demand of the job. She is exhausted from her duties at home and work, and her self-image is shot to pieces. She is afraid that because she has gained so much weight, her bosses will no longer allow her to handle customer interfaces. Her husband gifted her a gym membership but with all the new responsibilities she hasn't been able to use it; she does not even have the time to make herself a separate meal. It's just simpler to eat what the family eats, so a diet is not practical for her. She carries a photograph of herself from her honeymoon when she was at her ideal weight in her handbag. While she loves her child, she constantly wishes some things could go back to how they were earlier.

The trust we need to navigate change must bolster us internally and externally. Our instinct is to attack incoming change with resistance. This is as much a physiological response as a psychological one. The lack of certainty kicks our brain into survival mode, anticipating danger. When we can't see around the corner, our brain's job is to keep us safe. We are in fight or flight preparedness. We overestimate threats and underestimate our ability to cope with them. The stress response is associated with an increased heart rate, adrenaline changes such as poor digestion, loss of appetite, sweating, heightened pulse rate and increased sugar release. This is why most people greet change with anxiety. All the associated psychological emotions like fear, dread, anticipation, uncertainty and inadequacy along with a plethora of other effects arise with this.

In Joanna's life, the pivot of motherhood brought her its associated new responsibilities: an altered routine, an expanded family, and a changing body. It also pushes our mind into a defensive mode. Spiritually, it asks our individualism to widen and accommodate a collective perspective. Thus disrupted, we assume if we could only keep the change at bay, we would remain who we were.

We now approach the change as though it were the enemy. We throw an arsenal of preventive measures at it – from gym memberships to dietary restrictions and deprecatory self-talk. We rebel against support and interference in aid of our independence. We tell ourselves, 'This is not the way it is supposed to be.' The vision of 'what it was supposed to be' has altered in reality and we are living in that gap, determined to restore the original. We thought that when the new addition came all things would remain constant. We imagined ourselves living the exact same lives that we did earlier, breezing through work and home life with just one addition. We didn't expect such cascading effects. Those were the terms under which we agreed to change and now we find that the deal has not been honoured. This feels like a betrayal.

The introduction of a new element alters things materially, mentally and spiritually. Physically, it affects our sleep cycles, work schedules, our appetite, it exponentially increases our fatigue, throws our body clock out of whack, our stamina and capacity are consumed by more demands now. Our input to the body, what we eat, is sacrificed at the altar of convenience. Mentally, our financial goals, needs, expectations and wishes have transformed. We are coping with feelings of inadequacy; our identity has changed from the capable person we've been so far to someone who is constantly judged, and who is constantly racing to keep up with peers. We now have to realign our image of ourselves as mother, spouse, daughter-in-law or senior manager. As the roles we step into transform, who we identify as transforms along with them. Spiritually, our consciousness of ourselves as individuals is coercively expanded to an essential interconnection, and we witness how the actions of others impact us and vice versa.

So, when Joanne's mother-in-law is unavailable to watch her child, Joanne has to take the day off. This affects her efficiency and knocks her already sagging self-image. All of this accumulates resentment because not only has the situation itself changed, her control over it and the radius of impact has shifted out of control too. Where Joanne was once making decisions entirely on her own, now she must renegotiate the boundaries of control, giving stakes in it to everyone from the baby to the boss. She no longer feels like her own person. The battle to regain autonomy, the individual battling collective ownership, becomes the source of her frustration.

All other things cannot remain constant because every change we go through has ripple effects in all mind, body and spirit layers. If we want to anticipate the impact a change will have on us, we have to first break it down into these layers.

The birth of the new-born wave impacts every other wave in the ocean. It doesn't change alone. None of us do. None of us are isolated in our transformation. As the ripple effect of our change heads out, causing those who come into contact with us to pitch and sway, the ripple effect of others comes crashing into us too. We are, thus, collectively in a constant state of alteration. To imagine that we can control the surrounding environment while allowing a specific change to impact us is to seek to live our lives as mice in a lab under an experiment. We are not mice, and no one is drawing up cardboard lanes we can run along at the end of which there will be a treat.

Would we even want to live that way if it were on offer?

It is not like mice live that way in real life either. In fact we like to tell ourselves the human condition is unique. Our philosophies tell us the world is governed by laws of creation, preservation and destruction. We see ourselves superior to much of creation and other species, because of our ability to consider and know these truths. However, elementally, we are subject to the same laws, of creation, *transformation*, and destruction as all other beings. Except all other lifeforms seem to integrate their change far more seamlessly into their lives, with far less struggle than we do.

Preservation is an essential life force:
Take two lemons, cut them into quarters and leave them with a couple of teaspoons of salt in an airtight jar. This is an age-old preservation technique. Place them anywhere you like, in a dark cool spot or on a windowsill where it catches the sun. Observe the changes in the jar over a ten-day period. Are the lemons 'preserved'? Are they unaltered or are they gradually transformed? The lemons will release their juices, their skins will soften and turn brown. Texturally they will be soft and jammy. The, now preserved, lemons are forever altered.

What we call preservation, even in its most literal sense, is at best a controlled transformation, just one where we are the ones introducing factors to influence the outcome. Nothing remains unaltered or unchanged. We can leave an old building to collapse or we can take it down with strategically placed blasts. Left to themselves, our extra lemons might rot in the larder. By using ingredients that make them flavourful as they decompose, we create an intervening outcome, insert a detour on their path to organic destruction that is useful and palatable to us. We can put in support systems to ease our passage. We can choose to lean on others, ask for support, and create our own unique rituals for self-healing and integration into the collective identity. We can ease into the change from a position of trust.

This is not a way to resist transformation, but rather to participate in it and use it to our advantage. What we insert into the mix is what turns the transformation in our favour. It is up to us to **transform our transformation**.

Wait a minute. All of human endeavour is a triumph of resisting change. We build walls against the encroaching sea. We channel rivers, blocking their courses with dams. We prevent the march of ageing and disease with medicine. We resist societal impositions and choose our own paths against much opposition. Without resistance, women wouldn't have the vote, equal pay, short hemlines or the right to eschew marriage and childbirth for more fulfilling roles they see fit. We pit our wills against our bodies for the glory and honour of sport and fitness. We have become who we are by resisting what was. So how is resistance wrong?

And what is the alternative anyway? Should we allow ourselves to keep gaining weight even when we know it is unhealthy for us? Should we ignore our children? Quit our jobs? Just stay ill? If we do not resist change, what are we supposed to be doing with it? Surrender in these circumstances seems like defeat. World Wars and the Holocaust, genocides, apartheid and slavery have been countered with resistance. Revolutions have been wrought. Great horrors befell those who had their power to resist taken away. How can we not resist when there are so many dreadful situations that would unfold if we didn't?

The answer lies in what we are resisting and how we resist it. There are two kinds of resistance: **restorative** and **progressive**. Restorative resistance seeks a renaissance of what has gone before. Progressive resistance moves towards what will be.

Let's not forget every terrorist believes he is resisting the onslaught of a force that would devour him and his community. Countries, nations, communities, families and individuals who are caught up in restoring themselves to a glorious past are trapped in a vision of something they once were or thought themselves to be. At a time when things worked out for them, the environmental factors were in their favour, they were successful in what they attempted to build. They lived on top of the food chain, money was easy, their existence benefitted others, they received praise and felt good about who they were. They would like to remain there. They resent all the violent tipping points that ousted them from that position. They blame these external impositions – immigration, rising population, invasions, drought, famine, disease, formalized education, codified laws, intruding religious beliefs, other people's faiths, practices and what have you – for the alteration in their status. The change is thus otherized, caused by the other and inflicted involuntarily upon oneself. Change becomes the enemy. People indulging in restorative resistance are so caught up in the idea of ceteris paribus that they wish everything remains constant as they introduce outlier events. For instance, one country wants trade with China but resents the inevitable influx of immigrants that follows. When you open the door to change, you open the door to everything change brings with it. So we want fame but not its associated intrusions. We want money but not fiscal responsibility. We want freedom of expression but not having to defend our ideas. We want the isolated jewel of change, a choice addition in a controlled environment according to our choice and comfort levels.

Gratitude by mental elimination:

**This is a modified version of the original exercise developed by Minkyung Koo, Sara Algoe, Timothy Wilson and Daniel Gilbert (2008).*

Consider a previous impactful change in your life that occurred sufficiently in the past so that you can now look at it with the benefit of hindsight. It could be a relocation, a life event like a birth, marriage, graduation, getting a coveted job or even something unpalatable like a death or loss of an opportunity. Imagine that the event never happened. Now make two columns. In the first write in point form what you think your life would have been like without the event – where you would have ended up and what you would have done. Include the qualities you now have that you perhaps wouldn't have developed without the event taking place. For instance, sometimes a loss forces us to grow up and become independent. Write 'dependent' or 'sheltered' in the column (since the loss never happened) and consider the ways in which retaining those qualities may have influenced your life and choices. In the second column, write down what you see as the difficult but ultimately beneficial decisions that resulted from the event as it happened in reality.

Now at the end, write down a list of three to five things to be grateful for from the change that occurred.

Here's the thing: **transforming our transformation** is only made possible if we allow ourselves to be altered by the change.

We are only able to make it work for us if we allow ourselves to be impacted by it. Only then do we get to impact it in turn. When we resist and swim against the tide, we get pulled into a series of efforts that leave us insecure and exhausted treading water. Then we're fighting a losing battle to Make America Great Again and are left with Brexit. We're looking for rare jobs in an industry that is itself shutting down instead of adapting to new avenues, technologies and channels. We want the old way back when the way itself is disappearing.

Resistance in this case works against the natural progression of the current. The eye is always on an imagined and mythologized epic period of past prosperity, a past king, a past ruler, a past status, a once ideal weight, partner, role or frame of mind. And we are filled with anger at the influence that changed it all for us. If not for him or her or it, we think our lives would still be on that once fine trajectory.

Except it wouldn't, because agents are not perpetrators of change as much as they are instruments of it. They don't cause it, they deliver it to us. If each of us are waves, we are buffeted by winds and currents, tides and lunar phases, the spinning of the earth, the passage of ships, underwater tremors, the water spouts of blue whales and the play of dolphins, surfers and swimmers alike. We criss-cross each other's paths incidental to the changing trajectories of our own and knowingly or unknowingly influence each other. One person in a wet market in Wuhan can shut down global economies for the better part of 2020 and 2021. We can blame Patient Zero or see Patient Zero as a conductor of a tipping point that was an inevitable outcome of crowding, hyper-interdependence, illicit trade in wildlife, climate change, unsustainable global practices and unhealthy methodologies. It is arguable that change would have hit us via another Patient Zero on another day in another market. So it is with most of the events in our lives. The harbinger of change is often incidental to the change itself though their actions and words may seem pivotal to how it all unfolds. One wave collides with another in the ocean and the waves are incidental to the greater swell and sway of the ocean itself, manifested by a myriad influences that in a specific, non-replicable formula, create that unique instant. The conditions of that formula are unique to each individual's chain of volition, the cause and effect in their own life.

Hence, all efforts in the service of restorative resistance are set against the present moment taking place and a future trajectory unfolding. You're trying to prevent two waves in the ocean from colliding and changing course. Good luck with that.

Milind Gogate had come from a humble background. Having worked all his life in a cooperative bank he had completed his tenure with due honour. His staff felicitated him with a bouquet of flowers, and the regional manager honoured his years of service with a plaque and an expensive dinner set on behalf of the bank. He had in the course of his employment arranged the weddings of his two daughters and set aside moderate retirement savings for himself and his wife to live off. They had paid off the housing loan. Still, overwhelmed by years of work and now having nothing to do, no responsibilities to fulfil, at the age of 65, Milind fell into a deep malaise. He would spend hours sitting in his chair, dressed for work, looking out of the window. He stopped interacting with his friends and family. He longed to be 'useful' again.

We can become so invested in a fixed image of ourselves, something we have worked our whole lives towards, that even the milestones we've anticipated are not easy to confront. We are not nearly as prepared for what we think we have been preparing for because we have overlooked the violence of it. Change seems to sweep away the identity of our past. We look but are unable to see concrete evidence of everything that we once were. The river now runs underground and we are left thirsty.

When this happens in our youth we are able to restore faith quickly. We realize some things go but other things replace it. So we may lose a relationship or develop trust issues, but we quickly find solace in another relationship with a more loyal partner. When this happens at an age when we are vulnerable to loss, when very few things emerge to replace those that are lost, we return to a state lacking in object permanence and seek reassurance in visible signs and symbols of the continuum. Such a person may become clingy and needy, wanting his daughters to keep visiting him or his grandchildren to come to him with their daily lives or getting underfoot in his wife's fixed routine. He feels like he is becoming an unwanted irritant and slips into a self-deprecatory mental dialogue. 'Nobody wants me', 'I am useless'. Milind felt helpless. Working at restoring the past, regaining a lost era of skills, status and productive role became all-consuming and took him down a self-deprecatory and frustrating path.

Be your own rock star:

Imagine that you are the equivalent of a former film or rock star in your profession. You're at the end of your career and younger talent is coming in. You no longer fit in the industry. An awards function has decided to confer upon you a lifetime achievement award. A major magazine, like the Rolling Stone, *is sending a reporter to interview you. Visualize yourself summarizing your past glory and achievements to him as he writes them down. Remember that you're going to be on the cover of the magazine. As you speak, consider that this is the legacy you're going to be putting out for the public to see. Write the report on your life. When you finish writing, let it rest for half a day and then come back to it as a reader of the famous magazine. How do you come across? A man with sadness and regret looking back on his life or someone who has lived well and is looking forward to a new era? One who is clinging to past glory or one who is able to turn into a mentor for young, new talent? Do you sound like you've given up, telling young people to 'enjoy it while it lasts' or as an elder, still a leader in your own space, confident and secure? Read it out to a trusted friend or partner and ask them what you sound like. Then consider what you would like to sound like at the end of your career. What could you contemplate doing now that would make you that sort of a leader on the verge of retirement?*

When Milind stopped trying to return to the past, instead learning to use his past to impart wisdom and knowledge by becoming a guest lecturer at a nearby college, he found a new audience and validation for his lifetime of work.

The good news is that restorative resistance can be converted into progressive resistance. The actress Marlene Dietrich once said, 'Never confuse movement with action.' The difference between moving and acting is the difference between reacting and responding. Movement looks like we're doing things but we really aren't. We become satisfied with what fills the gap rather than with what propels us forward.

When we are in a constant state of reactivity, we are engaged in saying some words, making some noise and taking some steps to satisfy ourselves that we've done something. We go through the motions. All of social media is about feeding this need. We post reactive comments to feel as though we have done our bit without actually doing anything at all. Unless we first determine if the steps are moving us forward, all our movement is futile. We may as well walk in circles. To simply react is not to act.

Reaction serves no purpose beyond satisfying us that we've done something. On the other hand, when we use social media to connect what is available to people who need it in a time of lack, when we use it to verify, link, connect, collaborate, and collectively tide over the systems that fail us, we convert the same movement into radical action. As compared to a reaction, a response is focussed on outcome and fills the void.

Sometimes, reactivity can be a product of our fears and uncertainties. We react *so that* we don't have to respond. To respond we have to not just accept change but demand it, which is hard. It is easier to stay in our comfort zone and resist restoratively. That way the change that occurs won't have a workable outcome for us and we can say, 'See, what did I tell you? That was bad news. What has happened is just terrible. The good old days are gone.' It can also offer us attention, support, empathy and the companionship of others in the same boat. We find commonality in our commiserations and bemoan the passage of time and circumstance. The lack of submission to change insulates our pride, preserves our grouse and keeps us believing in the status quo. It becomes our secondary gain.

It can be lonely and frightening to take the steps to move forward because all change moves us into the domain of the uncertain.

Sushila TRS is a Hyderabad-based housewife who has put up with several years of abuse from her husband. Now that her two children, a son and a daughter, have gone off to college, she is alone with her spouse and finds that communication between them is at an all-time low. She wonders if she should stay or leave. Unlike many others facing similar situations, she is financially well off, having worked as a teacher, and has savings and jewellery. She also inherited her mother's house after her demise, so she wouldn't be homeless if she left. But she has become used to him. After all, it's been nearly 30 years. What will society say? The family would be upset with her. Moreover, what will she do on her own now? What meaning will her life have without her husband? She finally decides to take a trial run, a solo trip to meet her sister in the US with a stopover in Europe. She loses her passport, has her money stolen, misses her connecting flight and is stranded in a foreign country. 'See?' she says, echoing her husband's admonishing tone, 'I knew I couldn't manage on my own.'

A similar pattern of avoiding the steps to tangible change plays out in many ways among women who face abuse. We tell ourselves, we can't, we shouldn't and subconsciously are primed to look for the affirmation that we are wrong to.

Chellamani Gangadharan moved from Chennai to Singapore five years ago. Her husband is verbally and emotionally abusive. She has a 13-year-old daughter, who suffers from depression. She got a job and began to work, grateful for some financial independence and the chance to get out of the house for a while. She also managed to pay for personal therapy sessions in secret. However, her child slipped further into a depressive disorder during this time. Her husband blamed her, telling her it was because she was negligent, unhappy in her marriage, constantly complaining, incapable of fulfilling her duties or sustaining even in her new role at work, that her daughter was affected. Afraid that he was right, Chellamani quit her job, discontinued her therapy and remained in the abusive relationship for the sake of her daughter.

When what we have in hand is a certainty, however inadequate it may be, we tend to choose this over uncertainty, which we look upon with fear. We choose the status quo over transformation. When the goal is restorative rather than progressive, change becomes doubly hard. We choose the way things were before the abuse began because what they will be when it ends is inconceivable right now. The instinct is to aim to return to a time when we first got married, when we had hopes and dreams as a couple, unmarred by anger and resentment, before we had our child. We seek to restore a past that has long left us behind. We are turning back and being turned to salt.

With our body in fight or flight mode, our psychology is triggered to defend and our spirit fights the collective with individuality. The only way to calm things down is to change our relationship with change. We must move from enmity to friendship. We may not be able to change the probability, ambiguity and complexity. The unknowns may remain unknown. In that situation, we are only able to say, 'I don't know where this is going and I'm fine with that' and take those first steps anyway, trusting that change is a friend. This is hard to do. Many of us stop at the stage where we say, 'But where am I going with this?' and fail to come up with a concrete answer. We assume the lack of that definite destination is a sign of failure. We then ask ourselves, 'Is it worth giving up the known for the unknown?' To embrace change, we need to befriend the unknown. We have to be okay with uncertainty.

How do we make our peace with uncertainty? By evolution, we lean towards the known odds. But ambiguity serves the purpose of pushing us towards exploration. Research shows that teens have a high tolerance of ambiguity. Their brains push them to explore the unknown and take risks, sometimes to their own detriment. This is their way of mapping the safety of the world that will kick in to be a GPS for them later in adulthood. A teen with a terrible experience of risk would use that as a warning system for future endeavours. One who got a great thrill out if it might use it a trigger for more risks, depending on the mental make-up of each individual. As adults, we become intolerant of uncertainty when we catastrophize outcomes. We imagine the worst and amplify the negative. We balance this out with realistic goals, coping mechanisms and putting in external factors to support us. A risk-tolerant adult may have friends or a parent or teacher whom they can go to for advice and who would hold them back. When our intolerance for the uncertain is high, we fear the outcome more. The trick then lies in increasing our tolerance for uncertainty.

Celebrate a week of uncertainty:

This experiment will try to help you expand your tolerance exposure, especially if you find it difficult to deviate from the norm. If you're someone who never leaves home without a fixed plan, try deviating from the normal route on your walk. If you typically have a fixed order at a restaurant, try a different restaurant or a new dish. Attempt a blind date or try out a foreign language film if you're used to the same old, same old. However, don't head too far out of your comfort zone. First, evaluate the threat. What could you reasonably do that would not put you in actual danger? Are you overestimating or underestimating the danger? What would make you feel safer? The trick is to establish parameters and boundaries while you embrace the uncertain. You could pick a restaurant or a comedy or a dish after reading reviews, getting recommendations from friends or searching for high ratings online. You could pick safe and well-lit or populated zones as you walk. You could ask a friend to come along. Consider what constitutes a risk to you and push your boundaries ever so slightly and incrementally, such that when you take a bigger risk weeks or months down the line, you'll find yourself more open to it than when you began this exercise. Consider that some risk and uncertainty leads you to new experiences and ideas, and it could actually be a pleasant thing.

Think of the experiment like vaccination. We introduce ourselves to the very thing that's attacking us until we use it as an inoculation against itself. We use change to erase our fear of change. It's like using a thorn to remove an embedded thorn.

In therapy, the first step, the first session of the client intake is always devoted to determining our influencing factors and goals. This can even take a couple of sessions. Sometimes the goals we come in believing to be vital to ourselves are not the goals we leave with. For instance, while the immediate need may be to stop domestic violence, as with some of the women whose cases we have read, the underlying and more pressing need may be to build enough self-esteem that they have the courage to leave a violent situation. Stopping violence can be achieved through any number of means, such as calling for help, complaining to the police, self-defence or involving family members. Yet, many are unable to take any of these steps until they perceive themselves as deserving better treatment. They need to set boundaries such that they are unwilling to take the harm any more. In this way an underlying goal becomes more vital than the primary goal. Defining this core issue with clarity takes time and insight. It depends on us embracing the willingness to change. And to do that we have to drop our resistance, stop treating change like the enemy and increase our tolerance for transformation.

Change as my natural state, a meditation:

Close your eyes and imagine you are in the middle of an ocean. Feel the water slapping against your body, your head held up above the water to gasp for air, your legs are tired of kicking to keep you afloat. Feel the exhaustion that comes with the position. Examine any associated emotions, such as anger, fear, dread or despair. The ocean is heaving and tossing. Now open your eyes and list down the things you think you would need in that moment to save you. The answers may be a lifeguard, a life-vest, a raft, a helicopter rescue, a walkie-talkie call for help, a rope, shark repellent, anything. List as many as you can think of.

Now close your eyes and imagine you are in the middle of an ocean again. But this time imagine that you are a wave in the ocean. Feel yourself among other friendly waves. You are one with the ocean, you are born from it and belong to it. You are not a foreign object in a vast body of water, you are in fact the body of water, as vast and boundless as it. Feel the water slapping against you. Consider the uncertainty of where you are headed now. What does it feel like? What has happened to your legs? What are the emotions you are experiencing? What is their intensity? What do you anticipate and what excites or scares you? Often, people find that their dread has turned to anticipation of the unknown, and their fear to excitement.

In one case, change is inflicted on us. In the other, we are part of the change. When we are able to participate in our change, we become less afraid of the uncertainty. Change transforms from being the enemy of our status quo to a friend of our future. This is how to transform our transformation.

5

How to Be a Wave

THE MOMENTUM THAT CHANGE BRINGS ACTS LIKE A GREAT wave that carries us to our unknown destination. We can step into its force in a way that works to our advantage, or end up washed off our feet. Ideally, we want to be surfing the barrel and tops of these waves, coasting off a beautiful curve and landing on our feet. Or even if knocked off balance, at least having enjoyed the spectacular ride. Sam Bleakley, a professional surfer, likens coasting on the ocean to mindfulness, a coming to balance between the wind, currents, beach shape, wave types and lunar-tidal movements. It's an inner experience he describes as 'active, alert and intent on balance'. To flow with a wave requires oneness with the environment. It is not conquering the waves any more than it is submitting to them. It is to step into the swell of the wave and move with it. To embrace change we must become one with the wave sweeping us away.

The first step towards embracing change is acknowledgement. We begin to cope with change by taking ownership of the pain of it. The reason so many people have a difficult time moving forward when disrupted is precisely because they're trying to move past the pain. It seems pragmatic after a point to bury an event or circumstance, put it behind us and never address the issue again. But how do we leave behind aspects of our lives, people we have loved, homes that have shaped us, pets who were our companions, marriages that defined us or objects we were attached to for so very long? To hope for it to be done and over with is just another example of denial. In denial we seek to forget and we repress. When we repress we reject what change brings us. In rejecting change, we are defining ourselves by it despite ourselves.

A pain set aside is not really resolved. Long after we have forgotten the specifics of the event, the emotions it instigated in us linger. Feelings are energy, they never really go away, they simply transform. They just pop up again somewhere else like a gator head in a game of whack-a-mole. When people speak of accepting change, they speak of it like the first step, when in fact acceptance is often what comes after the process of denying, reasoning, bargaining, railing against and arguing with the facts of change.

To acknowledge change is to articulate the tremendous force that it is. It is to feel the loud thumping of one's heart and sense in its full force the fear, anger, despair, betrayal, panic or unease that the change may have unleashed within us. It is to feel the earth shake beneath our feet and grasp that we have lost our bearings. To witness the way in which it has uprooted plans and disrupted trajectories.

A lot of acknowledgement processes include journaling, writing or speaking our truth out loud. We scream into the void. To acknowledge is not only a verbal act. When we speak our reality out loud we ground ourselves, we locate ourselves in space and time, note what is happening in the now by making concrete what has hitherto been an internal crumbling. Articulating pain is a powerful tool to make loss concrete. 'I wanted to be this, go this way, but I am not, I cannot now' or 'I feel like my whole world has been torn apart' or 'I feel like everything I have worked towards is gone' and 'this is the sum total of my loss'. We may speak about the impact of the change to ourselves, if not to friends, relatives or a support group. It is to bow to the moment that is beyond our control.

All of us aren't good at putting our feelings and thoughts into words. Our acknowledgement can also come in non-verbal ways. We may paint, sing, play music. Or we may not. We sometimes acknowledge the pain by avoiding, shutting down and burying the pain, which is a negative articulation. What we are not talking about is what we are talking about; we are just using a different language. In order to articulate it fully, we may use other instruments – like our bodies. We may lose appetite, hair, weight or interest in sex, or we may binge eat and chain-smoke. We may feel hot, tired, sweaty or cold. Our resistance to change may manifest as headaches, insomnia or in other ways. Each of our bodies has a unique way of carrying the trauma of the change that is a scar of our personal journey. Unless we're paying attention to our body and its sensations, we are unlikely to catch the language it is speaking.

Acknowledgement of the pain of change is the act of becoming aware of the multiple ways in which it has an impact on us in all its layers – physically, mentally and spiritually.

Onions have layers, so do people:

Close your eyes and imagine you are a child or teenager forced to attend a dinner party or wedding event with your parents when you really don't want to. You could also alternatively be an employee attending the event of a boss you really do not like. You are all dressed up in luxurious fabric and jewellery or a nice suit, but inside you are seething. Consider how you feel at the time. Do you sulk in a corner? Do you go about pretending everything is normal? Even if you are making polite conversation with the host or other guests, are you enjoying it? Contemplate the difference between the outward and inward layers, between what you are projecting and what you are feeling. Now consider that you are on the outside looking at this idea of yourself. You are someone else observing what you are feeling and what you are projecting. These are your three layers. Do you observe that all three do not necessarily function in consonance with each other? One is frustrated, the other is joyful, while the third is neutrally witnessing the other two. Note the qualities of each of these as you witness them. Note feelings, thoughts, emotions, physical movements – reluctance, joyfulness, enthusiasm, slowness, heaviness – and where each of these occur. How do they manifest? You might note some physical sensations, movements or gestures, some abstract thoughts and emotions, and some sense of detachment. These are the three planes on which we function, but which we do not always note as being distinct.

When we do not know or like what we see happening, we are impacted physiologically. Think about an unpleasant occurrence in your life. Maybe what it felt like to be laid off or given some bad news, to have received a rejection or been passed over for a promotion. Then examine what the thought or memory makes you feel. You'll probably notice a tightness in the pit of the stomach or in your chest. A clenching of the jaw and tensing of the shoulders. A sensation of heaviness. Uncertainty leaves us with an increased heart rate, heightened anxiety and lower blood pressure, leaving us in fight or flight mode. This is the physical impact we note when we think of where we were when we heard some catastrophic news. We remember the physical sensation and the corresponding feeling. The fact that we remember it, noted it and are able to recollect it shows that we witnessed ourselves going through this as though from the outside.

This acknowledgement across three distinct layers is necessary because most of us try to 'be strong'; we don't want to 'wallow' in pain. Depending on the pressure of the situation, we may continue to act joyful while suppressing our feelings of frustration. We then attempt to 'move on' with the feelings unresolved. We don't go to our parents or our boss and say, 'I didn't want to come' or ask, 'Why did you make me do that?' We bury it and keep acting our part according to what the situation demands. We may also imagine that prolonging our consideration of pain, or 'wallowing in it', shows us to be weak. We fear that in our pain we are made vulnerable and to acknowledge that vulnerability is to be somehow publicly shamed by it. 'Oh get over it,' someone will say. Some might suggest we take ourselves for a jog and 'get some fresh air' or begin dating again when a suitable time period has passed. Such advice implies that we can do things to simply signal the end of the pain. That we can move forward without allowing ourselves the space to examine how much time each person uniquely needs to do this. Thus, we leave a vulnerable part of ourselves behind as we coerce ourselves forward. We each have our own time frame in which we become ready to begin moving forward. To absorb the full impact of change is necessary.

The reason this is complicated is because to acknowledge change, its pain, its whole impact, is not an active task. There is nothing for you to do. It is simply to sit in the awareness of the mutable moment. It is not to resolve it. That is a whole other set of steps away. To acknowledge is to gather the circumstance unto our bosoms and dwell over it and all the overwhelming feelings, surging emotions, bodily pains, twitches, and mental calisthenics that it invokes. To cite a mentor of mine and a fantastic psychotherapist, Ferzeen Faroodi, it is 'to just stay'. Just be. Just sense. Just witness. Do nothing, do not reject, do not embrace. To wish it away is to react, making it worse, leading us down a path of questioning, self-doubt, guilt and regret. Do not avoid, do not freeze. Just be. If there is anger, let it come. If there is grief, let it linger. If there is rage, let it vent. In the words of Zen master Shunryu Suzuki, 'Leave your front door and your back door open. Allow your thoughts to come and go. Just don't serve them tea.' It is to allow the emotions to emerge and present themselves with dispassion.

When we surrender to the emotion in this way, we are like newborn babies leaving the womb. We enter into the change kicking and screaming, our cries so vital to signify the start of life. When we are born and birthed, the uncertain passage done, we settle into a content cooing. The realisation that the new phase has begun brings relief and a sense of security. We are neither humbled by the transition nor inflated by its significance but quiver in equivalence with the process of change, not only shaped by it but also shaping it. It is to be born to the possibility or reality of what is. The anguish of childbirth is the significator of life. That is a powerful necessity of the moment. In it is the seed of all that is to come, including how one takes what has happened thus far forward. To be steeped in it is to comprehend it to fullness and allow oneself to be altered by it. It is to move with the surge of the wave.

This is how to acknowledge change.

The second stage of change is grief. When we have acknowledged change, planted our feet on the moving terrain with the skill of a surfer on a board in motion, we are able to then grieve for what has passed.

Grief is a necessary stage of expressing the acknowledgement of change. While we understand this for the loss of people or pets through death, we rarely apply the need to grieve the loss of identity, or the passage of key stages of life, or the things we leave behind due to change. This could be losing a partner in a divorce or a break-up, the loss of an important professional role or status, the onset of middle age, of positions and skills that have become redundant, the start of the empty nest period, or unexpected bereavements.

To grieve is not merely a lament to express our dismay, fear and despair; it is also to honour all that went before. It is to enshrine the past, which is not a leaving behind so much as encapsulating before we may move ahead from it. When we grieve we consider who we were in that phase. This is a delicate balancing act that calibrates the point from which we may move forward to become who we are about to be. It's the subtotal of our sum total, of what we add up to thus far. We also consider how we have arrived here and all that has brought us to this point, whether it is effort that now seems wasted or inputs from people and circumstances whom we must now leave behind. Hence, it is also giving thanks, gratitude. To grieve we set aside time to offer our attention; we honour the energy allocated to our becoming. We create a ritual or a rite, memorialize a space or a token that we imbue with meaning. We build up dedicated personal rituals around it that mean something to us. We need to do this periodically as a way of honouring our own journey. It is a remembrance of all that shaped us.

When we grieve properly and fully, we align our idea of ourselves with our journey. Then, our onward journey also becomes aligned. When we do not grieve, we become misaligned from that point onwards and whatever we seem to do doesn't fit.

Vasundhara was certain she was over an ex who would not make a commitment. She entered a new relationship thinking of herself as 'the person who is over the ex' and 'the person who was ready to settle down'. But as she went along, something didn't fit. It was not working.

Her ex began messaging her to say he regretted losing her. She was married now and her husband was a wonderful man, kind, patient, supportive and, above all, committed. She told him about the text messages so as to not keep secrets from him, and he reacted badly. He was hurt. She was offended that he was hurt. Their sex life rapidly disintegrated. She felt as though her body was shutting down and her husband felt even further pushed away. Vasundhara was hurt that she was being punished for telling him the truth and being honest. Her husband was hurt that he was being punished even though he had been nothing but faithful, loyal and committed. The nature of their relationship changed. And now, each nurses a sense of betrayal greater than the other. 'We don't seem to even know who we are any more,' Vasundhara says.

When we have unresolved issues, we have to pause, go back and look at the point of fracture, the point at which our layers began to separate. We have moved on physically and materially, but we have left a part of ourselves behind at a point of emotional breakaway. We will find here residual anger, fears and insecurities that have remained repressed. Our bodies internalize the rejections we have faced and this can manifest even when our minds seem to want to move forward. Because we have not resolved the stagnating past, we have not soothed its pain. This misalignment, as we go along, expresses itself in mind, body and spirit.

When we shut out the ability to grieve, we pretend to have journeyed on without pause from our tipping point. We have shown the world that we have it together. When we do not acknowledge our past and do not express our grief for it, we do not function in reality. The reality is a pain that when ignored, repressed or pushed aside can emerge as a backache or a shoulder pull, migraines or just an inability to commit to anything else; we live with it rather than address and resolve it. Anything that's denied or repressed will pop up at the most inopportune moments.

Rajesh Saklani is a warehouse manager in Indore. He wanted to learn to control his anger, which was earning him a bad reputation. His supervisor had told him it was preventing him from being promoted. He was so efficient at his job; if he only learned to control his anger, he would do so much better. He tried yoga, meditation and all kinds of techniques like counting to ten, drinking water or leaving the room when angry. But he still couldn't bring his outbursts of blinding rage under control. Finally in sustained therapy, he broke down remembering his father's passing when he was just a teenager, which placed the responsibility of running his transport business on his inexperienced shoulders. He barely had time to grieve. He had to grow up overnight. When the business tanked, he blamed himself for letting everyone down. He was angry at his father for dying and at the extended family for not seeing how much he was struggling. He needed to grieve his lost childhood, his formative years, the loss of career options and the different choices he might have made had he been given the freedom to. While his rage hasn't evaporated overnight, therapy has allowed him to come to terms with an entire range of suppressed emotions that have left him a very tightly wound man. He realizes that treating the symptom alone won't make the anger go away.

The eruption of emotion in your day-to-day life is a substantial part of your energy tapping you on the shoulder to say, 'I am tied up in something you have forgotten to address.' We will grieve inevitably, if not at the appropriate time, when it becomes too great a burden to bear further down the road. So it is required of us to return to the point of fracture and honour the pain of what we leave behind.

This is how to grieve our loss.

The third stage of change is realignment. We have worked on a past trajectory that we thought was swimming with an Arctic current. We were rudely interrupted by the warm Gulf Stream and now we are swirling in a pool that is directionless and circuitous. The question is: which way now?

Sometimes the answer to which way now is easy, sometimes it is not. Sometimes we can see our destination and just need a new way to reach it. Sometimes our original destination is no longer even visible.

There are three ways in which we suffer with our change – with material loss, when we get what we don't want or when we don't get what we want. All are problematic and we shall examine these in detail in Chapter 7. The first question, though, is how do we figure out what we want now?

Often the answer comes through the grief of the previous stage. When you have properly grieved and remembered who you are and where you are going, you have clarity. You may even realize why you were interrupted.

How do you realign when the road you were walking on seems to disappear from beneath your feet? To begin with, you acknowledge where you are, you grieve what you have lost. Then you ask: which way should I be facing now?

Nathan was leaving his small-town home and heading out to college for a photography course he had his heart set on. Around that time his father suffered a stroke and needed a full-time caregiver. It was expensive to hire one, so it became a tug-of-war between college fees and home care. His mother was not confident of handling the eatery the family ran and managing her husband's care on her own. Nathan, an only child, felt he had to be close by in case of an emergency. However, if he let go of the admission now, he wasn't sure if he'd be able to make his way back to college ever again. He had to choose between his duty towards his family and his dream. His destination was no longer visible to him.

Nathan felt he needed the certification. When he sat down to question his alignment, he began to wonder what about his profession made that certification so essential. Would it really matter if he just went to a college closer home? Who was the validation of the certification for? What if he did an online course? Then he was struck with the realization that he didn't just want any old certification, he wanted the respect that came with graduating from that specific school. Why? Because he felt left out when he saw his classmates join engineering, medical or other colleges whose degrees earned them respect, employment in good companies and high salaries.

His new dilemma led him to re-evaluate his dream job. What did he want to be if he had no constraints of relocation, qualifications and money? It was to be an award-winning photographer and set up his own studio. What were the things he would have to do to still achieve that goal given his constraints? He could begin by getting the technical know-how from a local institute and tying up with local news agencies to feature his candid shots of regional events. He would have to take risks and head out to protests, conflict zones, and get rare and unique images that the national media would want. Then, once he built a portfolio, he would have to pitch to be a stringer with larger publications. With the certification, admittedly, he wouldn't have to work as hard to be noticed, but in the end, he was still doing what he wanted to do and relying on the merit of his work for it.

Nathan could also accumulate several smaller certifications that would bolster his credentials. He could get into videography, set up a YouTube channel and vlog, use TikTok and amass a stream of followers. He had to challenge himself to grab eyeballs. What could he do to have a steady income and also save enough for college, which he could apply to a few years later? He could take on commissioned shoots at weddings, for modelling portfolios, and factory and corporate websites. He also thought of turning his father's small restaurant into a cooler café that he could man in the evenings. With a little investment in décor and upgrading the menu to attract a younger crowd, remodelling it as a student hangout, Nathan would be able to charge a bit more and increase his earnings per customer. The original goal wasn't completely erased, it just found itself at the end of a somewhat different path.

Nathan was still sorry not to go, but he was glad for the time he had left with his father. He felt responsible, like he was doing the right thing for his family. Mixed with the grief were feelings of love for his family. His emotional state was no longer black and white, resentful and angry, but bittersweet. Being armed with a plan to still make his dreams come true allowed Nathan to shift the college admission to the backburner and focus on the gains that would cumulatively outweigh the immediate loss.

Such a recalibration of where we are going only works when we have resolved the previous two stages, that is, acknowledged the pain and grieved to fullness. If Nathan had attempted to move forward without either of these, he would have regretted it either way. If he had stayed, he would always be resentful about giving up his dream and carried some lingering anger towards his father. If he had gone ahead and his father had passed in his absence, he would always blame himself for not having stayed home. Outcomes to each action, triggered by a cause he chose to act on, would erupt in various ways through his life, influencing the choices and mental states he would have to live with later in life, for better or worse. Staying in the moment and allowing himself to feel the full intensity of his feelings allowed Nathan to take the best path for him.

When we undertake the difficult task of processing our emotions and grief, we find our way forward to the existing destination with clarity.

We are brought to change involuntarily. But our move ahead from it must be voluntarily. That is how we take back the control from the suddenness of its onslaught.

We have a vision of an undisturbed whole that we had become attached to and that we protect. We work towards fending off anything that threatens that picture of completion. There is only one way to move out of the frame of regret – realignment – and that requires us to release our attachment to what we thought was our one true goal. Unless we do this, we are building an imaginary future with imaginary building blocks. Realignment is a taking stock of what is and where we are in the now.

Bring yourself to balance:

Vrikshasana, the tree pose is an exercise in stability and alignment. Stand with your feet together. Relax the tension in your shoulders and clavicles such that they are rested and not clenched. Let your chin fall softly such that your gaze is parallel to the ground. Lift your right knee upwards such that the thigh is parallel to the ground. Positioning the sole of your right foot against your left leg at knee level, pull the knee to the right side of your body to form a triangle. This will open out your hips and stretch your lower and upper back. As you place this foot also feel the pressure of the left leg that is supporting it push back against it. The combination of forces against each other is what will lend you balance. If the left thigh is slack, you will tip over. If the right foot is loosely set, you will tip over. Fold your hands in a namaste pose at the centre of your chest. The gaze, the hands and where the sole of your right foot meets your left thigh form your midline. Once you are balanced in your midline, you can spread out your arms and reach upwards like the outward extending branches of a tree and bring them to the folded position over your head, aligned with your midline. Breathe normally throughout the exercise. Vrikshasana helps you reach upwards even as you ground yourself in your present moment. You need to find a balance between where you want to go and what you have right now. You have to hold yourself to the ground, and yet, reach for the sky. The tree pose is also a pose of compassion, generating feelings of friendship and nourishment. It is a powerful reminder of caring for others even as one cares for oneself. Alternate with the left leg. Hold the combination of sides together for no longer than 10 minutes.

Only when we realign ourselves to what is available to us in our present moment can we see the elements at hand with which we may build a future.

The fourth step of change is **releasing attachment to a goal.** As the Zen saying goes, 'Let go or be dragged.' How does that make sense, you ask? All our lives we have been told to have a goal, focus on the goal and work towards the goal. But what if being attached to the goal is what is keeping us from the goal? When we're fresh out of college, we want to be the CEO of a company or the editor of a newspaper. When we're 35, we want unlimited vacation time to spend with family and friends, and we want money more than designation. Our goals change. Sometimes, we can be so attached to the one we've set that we refuse to see the joy of the one we're getting in exchange. We're also ignoring the journey. It is a better practice to examine what we are gaining from the goals we've set for ourselves and learn from those gains, letting go of our attachment to the original goal itself.

Goal inflation:

Blow up ten or more balloons and take them to your terrace or balcony. Helium balloons are good for this exercise, but if you can't find those the regular kind will do. Think of a goal you are truly attached to, the plans for which have been recently disrupted. It could be a qualification, owning your own home, relocating, getting married by a certain date, earning a certain figure salary, pursuing a love interest ... whatever is important to you. Contemplate what need is fulfilled in you by achieving this goal. It could be security, validation from the peer group, approval of parents, stability, companionship or a sense of achievement. Write each of these on a balloon with a marker. Now think of another way by which you can possibly fulfil each need. Is there an alternate way to get your parents' approval, achieve stability or become financially secure? You may even think of something that helps you release the urgency of a particular goal. Will another college do? Will talking to your parents help? Will a prolonged engagement or an informal commitment ceremony do instead? When you are able to think of even one other way to meet these needs, release the corresponding balloon. If you have any specific balloons left, keep them and contemplate alternatives or ways to release them or meet them until they are all gone.

When we work towards a goal, we lose the joy of the meandering. Think about it. The only reason we have to rue the loss of the trajectory is because it cuts us short of our goals. Remove the goal and we have no corresponding sense of loss, just a sense of redirection.

Wait what? Whaddya mean by release a goal? You *just* said that acknowledgement and grief gives us clarity and realignment allows us to set new goals! Of course, we're always working towards something, we have a general direction to our lives, what we release is then not the act of having or setting a goal, but the attachment to the goal as the *only* possible outcome of our paths.

If our aim to reach a particular point is the greatest thing in our lives – overpowering everything else in it, including our experience of life itself – it is setting us up to come crashing down soon enough. We see the truth of this when we understand that the essential nature of the world is Anitya, Impermanence, change. Change is the only constant, so a goal that is not adaptable is not sustainable. A goal that you will not, cannot change, is waving a red flag at the bull of change. We may reach some and not reach others, we may have to tweak the path and we may have to change the goal. We assume or rather, have been told that holding on makes us strong and being steadfast is a virtue. However, it is letting go that allows us to be dynamic in life. Rigid goals often also hide our own underlying and unspoken needs. We may not actually want the promotion; we want the respect that comes with it. We may truly not enjoy backpacking through foreign youth hostels; we want to feel cool in front of a peer group we admire. Nevertheless, we go ahead and put 'make it to VP' and 'backpack through Europe this summer!' on our bucket lists.

Aditya, 32, has never had a concrete plan for life. He didn't go to college after flunking out in twelfth grade and has never felt the need to. At school, he was brilliant at science but not so good in other subjects. So he focused on the things he liked and just shrugged at those he didn't. He was always to be found with a stall in science fairs, tinkering with electricals, plumbing and the internet. His family had coped with considerable loss in his childhood and Aditya internalized the lesson that even the most concrete goals can fall apart. So now he avoids making any.

His parents were quite supportive and let him amble along in life, though with hindsight, he does feel that he could have made better use of the first 20 years of his life. He completed a diploma in information technology while his friends were slogging through competitive exams and got a job. He set up the website for the company that employed him and brought in good business for them. Then he joined a well-funded but small unicorn start-up in a decision-making capacity.

He recently made the switch to a larger company, heading two of its divisions during the lockdown, and has felt some fear and nervousness. The new work culture leaves him with a sense of dread and sometimes blankness. The whole mindset in this company is foreign to him. He finds navigating the new ways annoying and has lost his motivation to work.

'I want to completely break away from it all and do something completely different and fresh, but now I am too scared to do it without financial backing,' he says. His single greatest gain with this change has been monetary. He knew the loss from switching to a more formal environment would be hard but didn't think it would be this hard. He compensates for his lack of a degree with dedication and confidence. 'I don't slack off, I can put in 16-hour workdays, and I have a certain amount of professional pride that doesn't allow me to fail,' he says. But his transition to the larger work environment has him in a spot where he is afraid to fail.

So far, he had the luxury of choosing where he would work depending on whether he would perform well there. His careful life strategy has been to use his freedom to avoid failure. Now he must confront the risk, and his old fears of failing in school have come rushing back, manifesting in his dismissal of compliments, which he doesn't like to receive. This time around, exiting isn't so easy because the goal has become important as he has climbed the professional ladder. Now attached to the goal, he must remind himself to take things as they come. 'It is what it is, I take it as it comes. If at all I have a goal, it is to get away from life as we know it,' he says.

Subconsciously, Aditya still carries the dread of failure and rejection that flunking out in grade twelve caused. His trajectory has been set by carefully setting himself up to avoid failure at all costs. When he picks only the things he is good at, he will never fail. But life has a way of tripping us up. Now he must confront the possibility of failure and it leaves him anxious. Aditya has neither acknowledged nor grieved all that he has missed out on in the last 20 years, the carefreeness of college life, from lectures, groups of friends, last minute studying for exams, infatuations and hanging out, early ambition, the social and cultural norms of moving through first jobs, and how one evolves through them. When he allows himself to, he will be able to take the same confidence that carried him past the challenges of his early life into his future.

We are all afraid of being judged by the standards others have set – people who work until retirement in one job are 'good', people in long marriages are 'steady', people who have done one thing one way throughout their lives are to be feted. They may be, but the longer we live we realize that longevity in business, marriage, society and family requires certain compromises that many of us are not willing to make or that do not suit us. We end up making these compromises with increasing discomfort in order to achieve these mythical must-reach goals. When we see this, we recognize that losing a goal is often not the worst thing in the world. A compromise is that which is weighed against one's freedoms – what you lose against what is gained. Some marriages are truly great, and some jobs are really fulfilling. But not all are, and people who stay in their situations for longevity rather than fulfilment end up tolerating things they don't want to. This is what is sold to us as 'compromise', a virtue of the steadfast. They have had to go through things like abuse, violence and soul-crushing boredom to fulfil that promise of reaching that goal – all the while wishing they could be someone else, doing something else. People who are unable to exit abusive marriages because they fear the disapproval of others have accepted the artificial measure of their happiness. To accept the myth of longevity as a lifelong value is as reductionist as accepting change for change's sake as a constant. When you are able to recognize the underlying motivations of the goals you need to meet, you can meet them in more plausible ways and by alternative means that work with the reality of your circumstance, rather than pushing against the grain of it.

Change does not occur on a whim any more than longevity does. We don't change because we don't know what else to do. We change because it is inevitable and unstoppable as a force in our path. We change because we either have no options left or the cost of staying the same will leave us worse off than the cost of the change.

The cost of change is as much a business principle as a Zen one. In business environments as people invest more money, more time or more energy into something, the cost of change increases. When change comes at us, it becomes too difficult to go with it. We no longer want to change no matter how attractive the goal may be because we are mentally calculating the cost of all that has gone before. So if I've put 20 years into my career as a journalist and should be heading for a certain seniority and perks that all of that adds up to, changing to a career in counselling and reinvesting three years of study to start at the bottom of a whole new field seems, on paper, pointless.

On paper. Which is the mistake organizations make. We are not all calculable on paper. In reality, the new course of study expands my horizons and capitalizes on my accumulated skills in the field, like interviewing people, language and the capacity to cope with people in difficult situations. It offers me a much more rewarding environment, one full of empathy and understanding. One-on-one time with clients provides instant feedback and a steady learning curve that gives me purpose at a time in my life when I need it. This course also allows me the flexibility of private practice, which further gives me the freedom to relocate.

So, on paper my former salary of over ₹2 lakh per month has been traded for an intern's starting pay, but in reality the freedom it buys me is invaluable.

In this way we acknowledge, grieve and realign. Aha, you may say, you haven't released the goal. You're still bent upon the goal, you've just tweaked the methodology.

Except now, we are not so tied to prestige, status, designation and the pay cheque (we still need to be self-sufficient and pay our bills, so maybe we'll do a side gig). Our goal in its essence, what it stood for, and the intent with which we approached it, has altered.

And this is the secret that anyone who has altered a goal knows, one that Aditya recognizes intrinsically even though he still struggles with it. When we arrive at this ability to alter the goal, we are no longer attached to a specific outcome. We have changed the precedent.

Until now, our precedent has been: if I keep on this route I will reach my goal. If I deviate from a route, I will not reach my goal.

Now our precedent is: I have deviated from the route and found another goal. If I deviate from a route, other outcomes are possible.

Now nothing is finite, or immutable; possibilities are open, new paths are available for exploring and we have achieved an openness that was not possible earlier.

As the philosopher J. Krishnamurthi put it, 'My secret is I don't mind what happens.' Now we are ready for that acceptance.

The fifth stage of change is **acceptance**. Acceptance isn't just looking at what is on its way towards us and saying 'ok, I'll roll with it'. Acceptance is not passivity or fatalism. You are not obliged to accept injustice. You can accept your valid feelings about an abominable situation. But acceptance is also not piecemeal. You have acceptance for some things and not for others. It's a broader philosophy of living and working with whatever may come. It is an equanimity, whatever may be at hand. It is not minding what happens.

When you have released the goal, you are now able to do what it takes to get where you need to go. You may need to undo things, redo things or count your losses and write off some things, you may change the goal, you may digress and find other goals. You are now there for the journey, not the destination. Acceptance is enjoying the journey.

One has acknowledged, grieved, realigned and released the goal and arrived at acceptance. Acceptance arrived at in this way is not resignation. One is no longer carrying the baggage of the past trajectory as a burden, but as an encapsulated valuable lesson. One is self-assured and confident. One has dealt with or is working on one's insecurities and fears, but one is no longer tripped up and slowed down by them. We are off on a happy jaunt through bylanes and pit stops.

A dream home project:
Imagine you're an architect and you are building your dream house. You first imagine the complete house, then you draw out the blueprint of the exteriors and the interior plan. You pick the land, the view, the orientation and the capacity. You choose the material that goes into the walls and flooring. You note the all-important load-bearing walls, the foundation, the roof and the replaceable utilities and appliances. You look at the sources of power, water and ventilation. You look at what needs to be renewed and what the expense will be. These are all what make a house sound. Now imagine that you are the house. Consider what goes into the different components that make you feel sound, secure and stable. What is your view? What holds you up? What will you have to renew and how often? What is your foundation? Where do you get your power and light and air from? Consider if you have accounted for the all-important components. Are there replaceable components that you are tending to a bit too much? And would you need to check the wiring and ensure it's okay? What would you need to add to your house to make it a dream house and allow it to last through your life? If that means trading up to a better location and view, well, then so be it. It's your house and you have to live in it after all.

When we're enjoying our journey we also cease to compare it to that of others. We realize our paths are unique. We realize the houses we're building are entirely our own, designed to suit our own peculiar needs. When I build my house I am absolutely going to turn the space with the best view into a soundproof meditating/reading/chilling space for one (the dog being an exception to that rule), whether anyone likes it or sees the need for it or not. You do you when you build your house. Most of us grant that courtesy to the buildings we reside in but not to our own mind, body and spirit. When we acknowledge, grieve, realign, release and arrive at acceptance, we are also accepting ourselves, our needs and the past experiences that have shaped us more fully. So, what we build now will be more aligned with who we truly are. This is how we know we have arrived at acceptance. Nothing in what we build now leaves a part of us out.

We cease to evaluate outcomes or successes by longevity, reputation and other facades. We look for value that is intrinsic and forward-propelling. We become more willing and able to take risks because we evaluate what we lose in terms of freedom, happiness, curiosity and resilience rather than only in terms of financial gain or material success. We become individually stronger, like boxers in a fighting ring going a couple of rounds knowing that we will get punched. We take the blow because we're here for a good game, not necessarily for a 'win'. We now know that losing to a good opponent in a high-quality match is as exhilarating as winning. Who we are, thus, transforms.

This is how we participate in our change. We allow our change to change us. This is how to be the ocean.

6

The Oldest Fish in the Sea

The fisherman was an old man now with one wish yet unfulfilled.
Ever since he was a boy, he had heard the tale
of the oldest fish in the sea.
The one whom nobody had caught.
Many had tried, but failed.
Men far sturdier than him had come back with tales
of how he had given them the slip,
how they had ridden through
great storms with trained crews, expensive gear
only to returned empty-handed.
Some said the oldest fish in the sea
was legend, a myth, was magic.
But the old man felt his presence in his bones and set sail.
Asking his family not to come find him if he never returned.
He weighed anchor in the middle of nowhere.
No rod in hand, no net splayed out, no harpoons hidden.
Days turned to night, froth to glass, spring to autumn.
Finally one morning, as the sun was rising,
the oldest fish in the sea rose from the depths.
'You exist,' the old man said.

'I do and I do not,' the fish replied,
'My father told your father the same thing.'

~

ALL PERMANENCE IS AN ILLUSION. THE GREATEST civilizations become rubble, their languages dead and their wealth lost at the bottom of the sea. All oppression is carried out for dominion of supremacy, race, class, caste and privileges. The turn of the cycle is inevitable. This earth was once ruled by sabre-toothed tigers and dinosaurs. All who rule the food chain will be extinct one day. By chance or by design, decimated either by a stray meteor or by evolution. Even the microscopic cells of our epidermis are replenished every 28 days. The very body we witness as our own is altered as we watch. Death is inevitable for all beings, and when we do not strive for the continuation of what we possess, we strive for the legacy of it. We are consumed by what quantifiable aspect of ourselves we will entrust to the next generation, seeking control even after death. We pass the illusory baton on with the belief that if we keep the line of succession unbroken, somehow we will achieve immortality despite our transience. And in similar fashion, our children will pursue their own mythical immortality too. The continuation of all tradition, rite and ritual is lain at the altar of this endeavour. Our unbroken devotion to tradition is a monumental tribute to our ephemerality.

The fish do not leave behind tomes on their brief lives. Nor did the dinosaurs. What we know of them we excavate through fossil and faeces preserved in amber and lava. We imagine that we are special, different from all other species that were so cruelly interrupted, and so deserve to tell an unbroken history.

We think, we remember, we preserve, we have free will and sublime spirit, we have mythologies, we have gods, we have purpose and action, we have domesticated other animals, invented, cured, created, and we have an understanding of mind, body and spirit that other beings do not. We, human beings, are unique.

And yet, at our lowest common denominator, we are the same. All our uniqueness will become ash or dust, the same as a mosquito's body would when it completes its lifecycle. It may have been a brilliant mosquito, the best of its generation, but we will never really know. The touch-me-not has as much complexity hardwired into its biological system as the seahorse, the elephant and the human. Elementally, the end is as equitable as it is inevitable. Knowing this, as the Buddha said, how can we quarrel?

Pare ca na vijānanti
mayamettha yamāmase
Ye ca tattha vijānanti
tato sammanti medhagā

People, other than the wise, do not realize,
'We in this world must all die,'
(and, not realizing it, continue their quarrels).
The wise realize it and thereby their quarrels cease.

– *Dhammapada* Verse 6, Yamakavagga, Kosambaka Vatthu
(Translated by Daw Mya Tin, Burma Tipittaka Association)

All pursuit of superiority is based on differentiation. All differentiation comes at the cost of our interconnection. As the world strives for more and more differentiation, we fall apart amongst ourselves. We are so convinced of our uniqueness that we forget that in order for us to be so, others must be less so. Our privilege is relative, we progress when we are ahead of others. We pay more for 'exclusive' brands, institutions, apartments, access that derives from setting us apart from others. We express surprise when a farmer's daughter tops a competitive exam. Or someone from an underprivileged background makes it to a top position. Our wokeness demands we applaud a rags-to-riches story, but our surprise stems from our intrinsic belief in the implausibility of it. The surprise is of the realization that if all beings had the same supportive environment, nourishment, advantages, boosts, resources and opportunities, they could perform as well or even better than we have. Knowing this, we still attribute success to factors like drive, hard work, merit, and luck and compete to be better than others. 'May the best man win' is an affirmation that those who win are indeed better men. We coach our children to be these better men, grab the limited opportunities, have confidence in the unerring truth of their superiority, and what that can beget in terms of achievement and legacy. In a world of true equality, one man's intelligence, application and ambition is worth no more than another's. For us to be unique, the world must inherently remain unequal.

This comes from a competitive superiority complex. Every war ever fought on earth has been fought for this purpose alone: that some may remain superior to others in idea, existence and legacy. When we examine the subconscious motivations that our need to be unique, to pull ahead of others, is built on, we will see more clearly why our goals mean so much to us.

All resistance to change stems from the affirmation of our differentiation.

The moment we cease to be unique, we have to cede our positions of superiority. We have to look around and recognize that we are no better than another being. If we are neither better nor worse, if our loss is the same, as is our accomplishment, what is it we are struggling for?

All struggle becomes meaningless. So also, all resistance becomes meaningless. It's okay if we give this opportunity up, it's okay if we don't have the biggest house, the best vacation, the Ivy League degree, the cool car, and the white-collar job. We begin to make choices differently, less from a fear of missing out or not being among an elite handful, and more with a view to enjoy and be fulfilled by what we do. We, thus, harbour minimal or no resentment against the goals and opportunities we do not claim or that others do.

When we witness our interconnection, this affirmation of uniqueness is what changes. The belief in our superiority falls away from our eyes, and we see with the lens of our inherent similitude.

We are sustained in the hamster wheel of life by the myths of our superiority. So none of the men who met the oldest fish in the sea returned to admit that it had all been a hoax, because participating in the hoax sustains their place in the lineage of great adventurers. We build the myths of our lives in this same way. And if we have put our faith in this myth of superiority our whole life, who are we and what have we done, what will we contemplate when it no longer exists?

We will contemplate Sunyata, Nothing. If there is no conquest, of mountain nor man, what in us endures? If everything changes, what endures? Nothing endures.

'Sab sankhara Dukkha, sab sankhara Anitya, sab sankhara Anatman,' the Buddha said. *All formations are Suffering, all formations are Impermanent and all formations are without Self.*

All our suffering with change leads us to realize that we cannot hold on to anything. **Anitya, Impermanence, is what lasts, is pervasive and interconnects us. To be able to see change as constant is equilibrium.**

We are the same principle, the same energy, manifest in all life forms. When we witness this interconnection, we see that we gain nothing in conquest. Also, we lose nothing in loss. Change operates like Einstein's principle of mass-energy equivalence that tells us with the right condition, energy transforms into matter and back again endlessly. We are in a constant state of transformation. In fact, from this vantage viewpoint, transformation is the only constant.

Our natural state is change.

When we are able to see that the natural state is change, two things happen: 1) we stop taking life personally. There is no grand conspiracy to derail us from our exalted goals. The goal is mutable, the path is changeable and we could or could not arrive at a destination based on the cause and effect in our lives and wherever else we arrive will be okay. And 2) we see ourselves as interconnected. When we are interconnected, we take pride in others' successes as much as our own, we feel others' losses, we become more compassionate and in doing so we invite compassion into our own lives. In loss or in gain, the journey becomes much more pleasant, palatable and supported. We no longer journey alone.

In our newfound ordinariness we are able to step out of the burdensome expectations we live with. To achieve, to carry legacies, to supersede. We are free to explore, learn, live, exult, laugh and even fail. A failure does not let down generations, destroy futures and devastate families. It is a goal that changed, a path that veered off course. We can now see where the new path leads.

Change moves from this abrupt obstacle to the cadence of life itself. We see that other waves in the sea are also impacted by a tidal rhythm. That while we each are pulled by our undertow, we share in the periodicity of ebb and flow. As we slam against each other in the cross currents, our paths become inextricably intertwined. And so, one by one, wave by wave, we become one with the vast expanse. You could not pick one of us out without unravelling a multitude of others over time, place and presence. As we become part of the collective, one with the ocean, we see the ways in which it sustains so much more of life than just us. We foster seaweed and plankton, anemone and fish in our depths. We harbour the big fish that feed off the little fish, and the birds that feed off them in turn. We see that we support cycles. Men take from the sea but send in sewage and trash, rake it of its harvest but never fail to receive salt, spray, vapour, condensation and rain in return. We see ourselves as a collective nourishing others as well as ourselves. We see that wherever we may end up, on this coast or that, whether we manifest as rain, or river, sweat or ice, we are not diminished by the forms we take because it is all one. We participate more fully in the lifecycles of our existence because we are no longer resistant and filled with resentment or fear. We are, just as everything else around us is, sustained and sustaining in the cycle of life.

We are not in the ocean, the oldest fish or the explorer fisherman.

We are the ocean.

We both exist and do not.

And as the ocean sways, so do we.

SKY

Nirodha, the Cessation of Grasping

7

Embrace Infinitude

A CHILD LOOKED UP INTO THE SKY AND ASKED HIS MOTHER what that burning ball was. 'That is the sun,' his mother said. By night, he discovered the cool serenity of the moon. He became obsessed with possessing both, each seeming to be a greater toy than anything he had in his cupboard. He tried many means to grasp them, jumping off roofs and attempting to fly off the branches of trees until his parents made the bonesetter a very wealthy man. His restraint lasted only as long it was being enforced. If his father went to work and his mother got busy with the chores, off he went again, reaching for the celestial objects. One day the Buddha was passing through the village and the mother ran to him. 'Please do something to cure my son of his delusions,' she cried, folding her hands, falling at his feet, tears streaming down her cheeks. The Buddha raised his palm in blessing. 'Delusion indeed, send him to me.' When the boy approached, the Buddha asked him, 'What is it you want?' The boy said, 'I want the sun and the moon.' The Buddha nodded. 'Sit here and I shall teach you how to meditate and if you do, you shall have them,' he said. The villagers who had gathered to witness this were stunned and at once distraught. Here they were hoping the Buddha would tell the boy he was stupid, but he was encouraging him. Nevertheless, long after the Buddha had left the village, the boy sat at the spot where the Buddha's feet had rested every day without fail, and closed his eyes. Hours turned into days, days into months and months into years. Every day his mother asked him when he came home, 'Do you have the sun and moon yet?' The children of the village taunted him, shouting, 'Hey, do you have the sun and moon yet?' Yet he meditated every day. One day, he didn't return home as he usually did. They found him at his usual spot, meditating. Days later, when he opened his eyes, he found a crowd gathered around him. They gasped. The sun shone from his one eye, and the moon, the other.

In the verses of the Dukkhata Sutra, the Buddha explains that the suffering of change arises in three ways. These are *dukkha dukkha*, material loss such as death or illness; *sankhara dukkha*, the rejection of loss, when we don't get what we want; and *viparinama dukkha*, the grasping for the gain, or wanting what we seek.

The only way to cease the suffering of change is to stop reacting to these three.

A message comes to you in your suffering: this ends. There is Nirodha, cessation. This is the Buddha's Third Noble Truth.

Non-reactivity is a tricky middle ground between pretending that suffering doesn't exist and being provoked by every trigger.

The way to deal with change is not to act like change doesn't affect us, we already know it does, but to reach a place where the pain it causes authentically ceases to bother us. This applies to what we crave and the pleasure we seek. When we respond to craving and rejection, we become puppets in the theatre of change, dancing to its tune. Our automatic thoughts, the first thoughts that flow when we are impacted by an event or incident, are our reactions. We can't just tell ourselves to stop reacting. It's a process to retrain this automatic thought pattern of the mind. We recognize that it drags us along the path carved out for us by the misery of change. We instead carve a different path out for ourselves, a space of stillness. When we arrive at this space of stillness, we will just be. Without rejection, without craving, without reaction and without extending our pain.

This is when we become elemental, mutable and yet paradoxically unchanging; we become the sky.

The process of retraining the mind is not an easy one. It forms the essence of an individual's lifelong mindful practice. It is a process of observation, concentration and meditation that inserts a pause between what happens to us and how we react to it. It is a harmonizing that each of us finds our own path to; it is our individual mental, physical and spiritual journey. When we find it, we experience change without being impacted by it. Just as the sky witnesses the weather. This is arriving at stillness.

Want it all.

This may sound counterintuitive but the way to overcome rejection and craving is to embrace all of it and more. Responding to a question on desire, the sage Nisargadatta

Maharaj challenged his students by asking them why they didn't desire more. 'Why not want it all? Complete fulfilment, joy, freedom?'

When we want small things, we are able to tell ourselves, 'I haven't asked for much.' And when we fail to get the 'not much' that we have asked for, we are able to say, 'And even that wasn't fulfilled.' This grants us what, in psychology, is called the secondary gain. It is the permission we give ourselves to remain in our status quo. Often we become comfortable with the situation we battle against. If we identify with the overweight, cheerful persona we have adopted, who will we be if we lose weight? If our relationship with a parent has been conflicted for over 20 years, what will our new relationship be after we resolve our issues? We fear the new so we stay with the old. Secondary gains are motivations that we have come to accept as our reality, or that we haven't realized keep us in a comfort zone, and they prevent us from taking decisive action forward. The change that disrupts us – the gym going out of business, our boss getting transferred out or our company laying people off – leaves us windswept. We use this as evidence that the effort change entails is not good for us. This allows us to validate our asking, 'What is the point?' This validates our choice to stay where we are, as we are and to consider the known position better than the unknown one.

When our goals are smaller, it only takes a minuscule change to disrupt them. When we become bigger, unlimited, expansive as the sky, small disruptions cease to matter.

We keep our goals small because we fear loss and rejection. When we aim for broader life goals – feeling fulfilled professionally rather than having a particular designation, feeling wealthy rather than getting a raise, feeling fit rather than hitting an ideal weight – a couple of things happen. We find other ways than to fulfil those goals, and we don't sweat about the small stuff.

Feeling professionally fulfilled, whether you are a chartered accountant or a teacher, has many more paths to it than simply getting a promotion. We could meet this need through volunteer work, holding remedial classes, maybe starting a social media channel for study tips and advice, giving talks, attending conferences, networking, writing a book, getting involved in research, working with NGOs and extending oneself in ways that propel us to become prominent and valued in the field of our expertize.

Then, if we are passed up for a promotion, it really is just one drop less in a bucket.

Further, these new avenues activate additional chains of cause and effect. New opportunities to progress open up, offering you even more ways to fulfil the same goal. Perhaps the promotion was important because it meant a bump in salary and a designation. You may start out giving free remedial classes for kids in need at the local Rotaract club and catch the eye of a prominent member of the club who leads you to more paid opportunities or to an interview for a better job.

When we take our focus off the immediate goal, whose circumference of influence is limited and defined, we open ourselves up to a vast scope of influence that remains undefined and full of possibility. When we cease to reject the pain and crave the specifics, we get past them with ease.

After years of suffering, Radhika was diagnosed with endometriosis at 27 and learned that she had complications which meant she couldn't have children at all. She was convinced her life was over. Radhika hadn't worked after college, having always planned to get married and be a stay-at-home mom. Now she was faced with an unavoidable emptiness. When she recovered from the trauma of the news, she went back to college and got her B.Ed degree, which enabled her to become an elementary schoolteacher. She spent a lot of time around children but still felt the need for more engagement. So, she began an after-school remedial class for children whose parents lacked the time or skills to give them a sound grounding in language and maths. Impressed with her dedication, the school management put her in charge of developing additional care facilities for underprivileged children. She retrained as a counsellor and went on to set up her own NGO, dealing with educational needs of the deprived. Through her work at the NGO, she met her husband and they decided to adopt. But by now, her heart had moved on from its original goal of having children of her own. She and her husband worked towards helping childless couples adopt instead. Bit by bit, working through her pain with therapy, she began to identify with all the children as her own, and this erased her deep-rooted feeling of lack. Without knowing it, she had taken up an exercise in sublimation, which is the psychological term for finding fulfilment for a particular need through another appropriate activity. Radhika and her husband eventually did adopt two children. She is glad that she did this only after she had reconfigured the idea of what having children means to her.

The undefined is uncertain. We may get great influences and opportunities or merely decent ones. We may get nothing at all for a while or not what we expected. But the key is to try more ways to extend ourselves. It may take days, even months, to build our reputation and get the kind of opportunities we'd like to have. However, when we are open to the uncertainty of it, we open ourselves to limitless possibility. With our original goal, we hope to be manager in a year. With the expanded embrace of uncertainty, we could be a best-selling author or a life coach setting up a consultancy practice in two years. Who knows? Unless we are able to release our limits and step out of their confines, we will never know what we are capable of.

Being bigger than our limited scope can be scary. In 1908, psychologists Robert M. Yerkes and John D. Dodson conducted an experiment on optimal anxiety, which has come to be known as the Yerkes–Dodson Law. They showed that being comfortable minimizes risk, but taking on a small degree of distress actually maximizes productivity. Simply put, the right amount of anxiousness enables us to perform better.

Stretch that comfort zone:

* *The following is a modified version of Yerkes and Dodson's original experiment. Find an open mic online or at a club, maybe in a part of town where you don't really know anybody or post a YouTube video of a performance. Recite a poem, do a small comedy sketch, tell a story or do anything you wish to. But here's the thing – tank it. Deliberately and pointedly underperform. If the thought of this makes you really nervous, do a micro version in your living room with friends, family and neighbours. Just don't tell them in advance that you plan to make it a flop.*

As you complete your piece at the open mic, observe the reactions of the audience and your own. The sinking feeling even though you anticipated it, the disappointment …what does it feel and look like? What do people say to you? What do you say back? Observe any physical reactions. Do you feel like crying? Is there a tightness in your chest, throat, shoulders, stomach or head? Give yourself a day's gap and then ask for a second chance to perform your piece if at a venue, or do it online. Note your anxiety before you begin, and this time, do a piece you know that you are adept at. Again note your physical and mental response after finishing. What do you notice about yourself that is different? How did not meeting your aim the last time affect you? What did it tell you about yourself that you didn't know earlier? Note that your aim was not to deliver a performance. It was larger, to gauge yourself as a performer. Ask yourself how you would have taken your 'defeat' the first time if your aim had been to be applauded as a great performer. What is the difference the change in perspective going in has made?

The sky is not concerned with how stormy it is in one part of the world because its perspective is much larger. It steps back and takes in the landscape of the earth in its entirety, and knows it pervades over it all. This knowing bestows a sense of security and ownership in one's calling. Things cannot be taken away from us when we live in this sense of expansiveness.

Think of the world as your home, and yourself as a child in it. You want the cookies but your mom says, 'No, that's enough!' So you wander off to watch TV, but find Dad's watching the news. So you go play. It's okay. There are other goals and other things to do right now. When you are secure in your home, the taking away of one treat or another desire is not the end of the world.

When we have object permanence, an approach of trust and security, we know what is meant for us will come to us. If it is being withheld, it may be with reason and for a purpose we don't know yet. Maybe dinner is better for us and yummier than cookies will be. Maybe we're going to go swimming in the pool, and we can't do that after we've been snacking. We have a problem with the loss of our goals when we lack this sense of security. We throw tantrums out of fear and the misplaced belief that only that particular goal can fulfil our needs. Larger goals are lurking around the corner, we just need to expand our perspective to notice them. Our frustration, anger and sadness arise from being unable to see the far-reaching abundance that is in reality available to us.

We also often confuse the means for the goal itself. We mistake the job for our goal of stability. The job is dispensable and may be thwarted, stability is not.

When we know that the world is ours, the smaller goals, of wanting this and possessing that, pale in comparison. Change that seemed a monumental obstacle isn't so much a boulder on the path as a pebble now. The trick to not being impacted by the fallout of change is to play the long game. It means we don't have one major goal that can be easily deranged by smaller failings. It means that we don't become so attached to a specific goal such that we cannot alter it. It also means we go to the core of our aims, rather than seeing the material gains that help us achieve them as the point. The things we do to achieve our goals now only become means, and not ends in themselves.

A stray meteor hurtling through space does less damage than a stone flung inside a room. Expand the size of your room. The solution is go bigger. Go so big that these smaller stray missiles that dislodge you on your way to achievement become too insignificant to obstruct you. Everything in the world, and if Elon Musk has his way everything beyond it too, is out there for the grasping. What is limiting your vision?

This is a lesson that applies as much to life partners as it does to financial goals. When we become too attached to one singular definition of what achievement looks like to us, we are limiting ourselves and shutting out other possibilities.

Delink effect from cause. How do we work towards something if we don't aim for it?

In 1972, Walter Mischel led an experiment at Stanford University in which he offered 32 children small rewards in the form of marshmallows or pretzel sticks in controlled lab conditions. Each child could have one if they took the offer now, but two if they waited indeterminately for the experiment supervisors to return and hand them their rewards. Follow-up examinations found that the children who had waited achieved better life outcomes, their SAT scores being one of the criteria for the conclusion. The ability to wait for our rewards, delayed gratification, was found to be influenced by factors ranging from BMI to educational background. However, researchers also found that waiting for the rewards led to increased frustration levels, as the children took to distracting themselves and falling asleep to bide their time. We experience similar frustrations when our life goals are in sight, but seem unreachable.

The Stanford marshmallow experiment is a teaching tool often used to explain delayed gratification. When we wait, we get greater rewards. However, there are many people who know that the reward doesn't always come and it is not always just. The example may be true for those who have established object permanence. But what of children who have grown up in poverty, whom life has taught that you have to grab the opportunities when they present themselves or you may not get another chance? We've all missed opportunities because we were waiting for a better choice that never came around, be it job offers and pay hikes to relationships and the one that got away. So, while delaying gratification allows us to increase our exposure to risk and calibrates our expectation of reward, it does not help us cope with the frustration we feel when things are not going our way.

Sometimes, life can feel like an endless string of these missed opportunities, so many of them not our fault. Often we lack the privileges others seem to have, like stable incomes, access to opportunities, trauma-free lives, resilience, comfort and care. And when an opportunity is presented before us, it's hard not to feel attached to the outcome when it means just so much to us. It matters, of course, every goal matters, especially when we think much of our future success depends on achieving it. It is a privilege to be able to feel that an outcome won't matter. It is the wealthy who are always saying money can't buy you happiness.

Being asked to go along with the change that comes our way even when it is devastating to us can seem like we are succumbing to an unfair vision of the world. It can feel like defeat. We are being told we don't deserve happiness or that we don't get to meet our goals, realize our dreams, and have stability, insurance and protection against the vicissitudes of life, in the way that others do. We also want and deserve to have a soft place to fall.

Coping with change does not have to be about self-denial, it can be about realignment. We can discover that, that which we source our happiness from isn't fixed. That there are other resources available to us than the ones we identify. That our options for success are not limited. That the things that block our way, from politics, rivalry, bigotry and prejudice, don't have the power to end our journey. That there are other paths to our goal than the one that is blocked to us. That we can, in fact, succeed without the validation we have been waiting for from those who withhold it from us.

When we are able to step back, release our attachment to that goal such that we open ourselves up to uncertainty, we may give ourselves the space to discover that the goal isn't the reward we thought it was going to be. There are other paths and other goals, other rewards and awards.

Our dissatisfaction comes from the thought of all the work we've put into achieving this one. Considering all the effort, time, energy and patience we spent on a goal, truth be told, we sometimes feel like fools for believing in the outcome. We feel cheated. The wait for the reward is interminable and frustrating. Like the children who gave up the first marshmallow for the promise of two, we have all sacrificed something, whether it's our time, relationships or other options, to pursue this reward. 'So close,' we think, 'almost there,' and something changes. We are cheated out of what we deserved.

Prathamesh was being bullied by his boss at the real estate company where he worked. He was shouted at, given menial work like filing and report writing, and was generally treated poorly. He was looking for another job but couldn't find one. He was too afraid to complain to anyone about his boss, who was influential, had been with the organization a long time, and a favourite with the upper management. So he bided his time and kept working hard. However, nothing he did seemed to be enough. He really needed the job to pay his EMIs and was hoping for a raise that year. One day his boss called him into a conference with senior management and complained about his performance and 'insubordination'. Her comments would go on his permanent record despite his having achieved specified targets. Prathamesh realized nothing he could say could put him in the good books of his boss. He patiently heard the management out and asked what he could do to change their perception of him. The senior executive asked him to put in a certain number of extra hours over the next few months, until the financial year closed. This would mean even working weekends during the peak season of their operations. Prathamesh agreed to do so but requested that when the season ended he could be transferred to another department. The management gave him their word, but Prathamesh felt defeated. He was convinced he would be fired when the term of his 'deal' came to an end, and made plans to wind up and move out of the company. Instead, the senior management appreciated his uncomplaining diligence. He was transferred as promised. They found him a role in the research and analysis wing where he could work independently and under a much more appreciative supervisor. It wasn't his exact field of expertize, but here he was challenged to learn new strategies and roles. While he was junior to a lot of others who had more specialized statistical skills, he had space to grow. And it turned out he became most prized for his ability to keep his cool when working with difficult people and was entrusted with negotiation roles between different teams. Management also granted him a fund to get the data and statistical skills he needed through a part-time course he could do alongside his work. Now every time he meets his former teammates in the canteen, they tell him how lucky he is to have made the shift.

The linking of the goal to effort is a pattern ingrained in us from childhood. We are taught this in many ways, from mothers who tell us to eat our veggies to be strong or to study hard to do well in life. However, part of becoming an adult is the realization that things don't always work out in a straight line. Many random factors, called conditions, intervene, changing the course of the outcome from what our intent was. We've trained hard for a match but had the weather or our bodies turn against us. We are constantly subject to outliers that introduce the drivers for unexpected change.

Seeing the goal as something we deserve, a reward for our hard work, a straight line connecting effort and reward, serves up resentment.

Pooja, 39, worked for a mainstream media organization and found that while she enjoyed the job, worked hard and reaped the rewards, her health, time and energy were being compromised. This began to take a toll on her, and with the urging of her family, she decided to quit. There was some lingering fear at the uncertainty of what lay ahead, and some resentment for the effort she had put in over the last decade that would now go to waste. 'I was on a straight path. I knew what the outcome was going to be,' she said. It felt frustrating to have that taken away. But she also felt enthusiasm for what the future would bring. The hardest part was the income loss that felt like a loss of autonomy. She was now dependent on her partner for her expenses and, while it hasn't created any issues, having been financially independent for so long, it irked her from the inside.

She needed to reconfigure her comfort zones. The change however brought her some welcome latitude. She went back to take an exam she had failed 15 years ago. She updated her content writing skills to stay relevant. She learned how to talk to clients. She cut down her expenses and became more frugal. She learned to cook decent meals. She still hasn't come to a resolution. Uncertainty is still her norm and she keenly feels the need for a guide. 'I wonder about whether I should be doing more of one thing or the other, investing my time in one path or another way. I have no recourse but to rely on my internal compass. I do feel the need to build my confidence,' she admits.

Cause and effect are a fundamental truth of life and, ideally, we'd all like them to offer us a straight and narrow path. I do this, I get that. All action elicits a reaction. So how do we delink the two? We separate them by inserting a pause between them. When we become mindful and meditative, we are able to witness the causes that drive us in ways that haven't been apparent to us before. We see the endless cycle of reactivity this pushes us into, one cause setting off a reaction that becomes the cause for another and so on. We see this pattern of fear, despair, anger and frustration replicate across the course of our own lives, often pushing us into saying things we wish we hadn't and doing things we wish we wouldn't. We've used paths as escape routes out of reactivity instead of making discerning choices out of responsiveness. Cultivating a pause allows us to remain equanimous, neither going overboard with our expectations nor believing the worst of humanity.

Let us for a minute entertain the possibility that if we receive more than our fair share of change, we receive disproportionate windfalls too. When it comes to what seems punishing in life, like change or disruption, we tell ourselves that we have received a strict measure. That if only we had done or not done an action, we wouldn't be in this position. But we are much harsher on ourselves when we do the math of cause and effect, effort and reward, and crime and punishment in our lives. We think of fate, the universe, God or whatever belief system we follow as this hard, exacting task master who's sitting there with a calculator, noting the days on which we don't show up for life, and taking our goals from us as punishment. This is an entirely man-made notion of justice that seems more like a vengeful prison camp warden. Life isn't quite so exacting or calculated in its system of handing out hard exits, punishments and rewards. We do get disproportionately knocked down by the hard parts but we also do sometimes get a great hand up. Sometimes it's hard to tell which one is coming our way, so we are surprised when the change shows up. What's important to remember is that whichever change we are currently experiencing, it too is Anitya, Impermanent, and cannot last. These causes and effects create each other and flow into each other. When we are having a bad day or making a decision we haven't really thought through, we can end up with some not so desirable effects. The good news is, when we are conscious of this, we can sow other causes to reap other effects.

We also gain clarity on the distinction between the means to the goal and the goal itself, which allows us to look at the processes as dispensable and replaceable.

Have SMART goals:

**The following exercise is based on William Glasser's Choice Theory or Reality Theory (1965).*

Collect five boxes/tins, one each for the five human needs – survival, freedom, fun, power and love/belonging. Write down the things in your life that help you satisfy each need, even if with some difficulty, and whether you like them or not. For example, it could be a job you really dislike, but it helps you survive. Now, take each box and map each thing you put into the box against the SMART checklist. Is each process you're undertaking to fulfil your needs SMART (Specific, Measurable, Actionable, Realistic and Time Oriented)? If they are not, what could you do to have an alternative to the goal at hand? For instance, if journalism is your bread and butter income, but the industry itself is in shutdown, is it realistically and actionably going to meet your survival needs? And given the pay cuts, by when? What else will help you do that? Have you mistaken any of the means you are using to fulfil your needs for goals themselves? For instance, have you started to think of being a journalist as your goal or is it a means to survival? Or does it now fulfil another goal, like power? Look through each box and separate the things you do to fulfil the need from the goal itself. How can you separate them? If some boxes are empty, what processes can you adopt to meet those needs?

Today, faced with change, we can delink this rigid pairing of cause and effect through mindful analysis of our true motivations. When we move to the Ocean pattern of acknowledgement, grief, release, realignment and acceptance, we break away from the established sequence and choose an outcome more suited to our needs. In doing so we break the link between our effort and the goal.

When we see our goal as incidental to, or one of the many possible paybacks of hard work, we open up a network of pathways that lead to the goal or to other goals. We open up to possibility. We eliminate some goals easily as we move on to others, while being open to what may come. The lack of a specific goal now has not ended our journey, it has merely eliminated itself from the running in our lives.

This is a form of delayed gratification. We are still forgoing the marshmallow, sometimes involuntarily, for what comes next, except we are not defining what is on offer. We're looking at what may come and evaluating if it works for us.

See that you stand at a confluence of conditions.

In 1998, J.J. Gross's Process Model found that it is typical to want to regulate our emotions by suppressing or controlling them. But when we used acceptance to regulate our emotions, we didn't change what we felt, but received the feelings without trying to control their quality, strength and length or frequency. The model found two key characteristics of achieving acceptance: willingness, which is our ability to step back from our emotions and not evaluate or intervene in them, and being present, which is embracing the moment in all its influences and factors.

Our disappointment is proportional to how much of a reward or outcome we expect for our work. The higher the seduction of the end result, the greater our anguish and the more we have to divert ourselves from the pain. Some of us self-medicate, distracting ourselves from the moment with alcohol, drugs and other forms of self-numbing ranging from binge-eating to video game addictions or social isolation. It is easier to see change as the enemy than to confront all the pain we experience. We feel attacked and when that happens, we take up self-protective, self-comforting and defensive postures.

How can we stop feeling this way and move to befriending our change? It helps to have a slight change in perspective.

Alka Godbole, 41, undertook a voluntary change when she chose to convert to Christianity at the age of 30, but it was the outcome of so many involuntary changes that preceded it. She was filled with fear, enthusiasm, joy and uncertainty. She hadn't been 'brainwashed' or 'led astray' as her family claimed. She had been a victim of sexual abuse as a child, and had found refuge in the faith through personal reading. She had spent a couple of years in enquiry and seeking before she discovered a church and community to engage with and that she wanted to be accepted into. She escaped her small town and found a place to stay at the YWCA in Mumbai. She found a job in a call centre, and claimed her independence. Free from the shackles of home, she began to explore her sexuality and came to terms with her identity as a lesbian. She could not come out to anyone. When she had left her small town home, her parents had been convinced there was 'a boy' to blame for her leaving home; her friends expected her to get married soon enough. She was afraid that coming out to them would take away the excuse that was actually serving her purpose. She was on her own. The process of coping with all these changes, her trauma, her sexuality, her identity, her faith, became too difficult for her and she began to suffer from anxiety. After struggling with it for a while, she decided she didn't want to undergo the change on the sly and told her family. Her father held a knife to her throat and wrote her out of his will.

Trust was a major issue for Alka. While on the one hand she was putting her faith in God, she couldn't bring herself to trust in people. She went through a period of great fears. These manifested as clinginess and exaggerated dependencies on people, and the need to please everyone. In time however, she changed her job, and after a period of dating, found herself a stable committed partner. She even came to terms with the fact that the church community that she relied on so much for her emotional anchoring, frowned upon her for being a lesbian. She managed to eventually make peace with her parents.

There came a turning point, Alka says, which allowed her to step back. It's not that all her fears went away. Instead, she was able to handle them better. 'I had the observation that even if I mess it up, God uses the mess to work his agenda through my life,' she said. Alka found that every apparent disaster was leading her to the person she was meant to be and to the place she was meant to be at. The acceptance also came with relief. She was learning that even as she was being sent here and there by multiple influences, she was going to be okay.

This realization was enhanced by looking back and noticing the choices and opportunities that had come serendipitously to her. She had graduated as a pharmacist but found a job at a BPO when she'd first left home. She had then retrained in finance. 'My first experience was not a mountain experience, it was a valley experience. But I learned to see that an important part of my identity came from my messes,' she says. She found purpose through her work.

Personally, she moved from being a dependent personality to an independent one. She went from idolizing and people pleasing to valuing herself without needing constant approval. And her absolute distrust in people turned into trust in herself. Above all, she ceased to define herself by one event or a set of events in her life.

Trauma comes to us from so many sources, as does our joy. It is hard not to feel targeted and victimized. And yet those who survive deep tragedies teach us, it is in refusing to allow oneself to be defined by one trauma or the other that we graduate to taking our power back. When we develop a perspective that is open despite the worst that has happened to us, we see small paths open up to bigger avenues. We attune ourselves to our more expansive goals and begin to recognize the harbingers of change.

We observe that the instruments of our change are incidental, and the change that is unique propels us on paths that work for us, one way or another. We end up in very different places from where we had planned to be and we find that we are okay in a very different landscape.

Recognize your driving factors:
Request family or friends to help you out or make a mental picture. Arrange chairs as though they were bus seats. Keep one ahead for the driver (that's

you) and the remaining behind you separated by an aisle. If you have people around assign them acting parts – a teacher, a mentor, a boss, a parent, a friend, a sibling, a grandparent and so on. If you are alone, just write these roles on chits and pin them on the chairs so you know where everyone's sitting. Take the driver's seat and imagine you are driving to a fixed destination. Now, have each person call out a different direction or instruction as you drive. These would probably sound like go left, go right, don't go there, go here, hey you missed an exit, you should have taken the other route... While this happens, think about where you want to go. Whose voice are you most likely to listen to? How distracting are the voices when you drive? Do the voices giving you instructions actually know the route or do they just assume they know? What other obstacles can come up as you drive? What do you have to do to shut out the voices and keep driving? If you did go on a wrong route would it be hard for you to reverse? And finally, are you enjoying the journey or is the destination everything? Would it be so bad if you ended up somewhere other than originally planned? What would make it okay, funny or adventurous even to end up somewhere else?

When you take a broader look at how our lives work out over a span of say, 80 years, losing a job or a marriage at the age of 38 is a speed bump on the highway, put there to change your path and slow you down. We don't always remember the grade we didn't get in school, the team that didn't pick us or the university we couldn't get in when we were 19. But at that time we probably swore we would never recover from it. What we're going through may seem life-changing in the moment, but it won't always be that way.

Recognizing Anitya, Impermanence, that nothing, however unbearable it is, lasts helps us see that we have got through pains that seemed catastrophic just fine, and that we will survive our losses just as so many others around us do.

The grief of others shows us this is the way the world is for everyone; we are not alone in this struggle. Which is why it is said that the best way to get over your own grief is to help others get over theirs. Outreach is not only designed to distract us from our own pain, it also enlightens us that our own pain is not unique; such suffering is common to all of mankind in some form or the other. When we nurse our wounds as unique to our condition, it is easier to feel deliberately wounded and particularly targeted. When we work with disadvantaged children, terminally ill patients, survivors of human-trafficking, people with disabilities, addicts, the homeless, the unemployed or the elderly, we realize our pain is no greater or smaller than the unspoken pain of others. When we recognize the commonality of suffering, the ordinariness of being, we become less special to failure or loss. Being buffeted by change seems less personal and we realize that this suffering of change is the cycle we all have to pass through.

We become windswept when we believe we are essentially altered by each passing storm. We are able to cope with change when we witness it as a fundamental truth of our lives. As things come to us, they pass away. And better or worse times will come and go too. And we will survive through them all. All of us will. Because the misery of the world is not ours alone. In our compassion, in our reaching out, in our interconnection, we are a world in need of deep healing from each other. And every bit we give takes our focus from our pain to that of others who suffer like us. Every bit of giving makes our own rejection and craving smaller.

Attune to synchronicity.

Swiss psychiatrist C.G. Jung proposed synchronicity as an acausal connecting principle. That which by its absence shows us the value of what is present. Jung said, we look at the 30 spokes and call it a wheel, but it is in the gaps between and around the spokes that the wheel's utility lies. The Sunyata, nothingness, is the bearer of the value of what is. What is eliminated shapes the path. What a sculptor removes from the stone is what makes the statue. Our utility becomes apparent in our gaps, in what we are not and what is not visible to us. There is no outline of the statue in the stone before the sculptor begins to take a chisel to it. We know these gaps, these absences by our intuition.

There have been many psychological studies of intuition. Joel Pearson, a researcher at the University of New South Wales, found that intuition does help us make faster and more accurate decisions. While some think intuition is the ability to make a judgement without express analytical reasoning, others counter that reasoning is there, but it is so rapid that we don't notice the process of analysis. Pearson found that subjects used subliminal messages, emotional cues and triggers, and used the unconscious information in the brain when they relied on their intuition.

When change occurs, we experience a paralysis of emotion, energy and action. Our path is cut off and we are unsure of which way we need to travel. Jungian approaches in clinical settings helped clients overcome negative thought patterns they were stuck into by deriving direction from external seemingly random coincidences. These worked as affirmations that they could move in a certain way. Jung found that one could train one's intuition using methods of concentration. Modern applications in mindfulness training also help increase awareness of this rapid subconscious analysis of patterns around us.

We can mindfully raise our awareness of our immediate environment, the sensory inputs it provides us, our thought patterns and our corresponding emotions. This leads us to see ourselves more acutely in context. We witness how small changes in the environment, our sensory inputs, cue our reactions. We assimilate body and mind into the flow of cause and effect. This allows us to see how we participate in change more clearly.

When Sameer joined the television industry after years in theatre, his main goal was to be a romantic lead in films. He applied for many roles but was told that he was simply not good enough. People offered him character roles instead. At first his ego was quite bruised. He had always been told he was excellent, had amazing skills and always outshone other performers in all his plays. So what was the problem now? He kept trying and received multiple rejections. When he reluctantly took on the roles he was receiving, he never really put his heart and soul into them, still hoping for his dream role to come along. After about four years he realized it wasn't going to happen, and he began to embrace the roles that were coming his way. He took the character roles more seriously and became so good at them that he was offered to play the primary villain opposite a leading television star.

He gained the reputation of being affable, accommodating and putting his best into whichever role he played. More producers and directors wanted to work with him. As he stopped chasing romantic leads in film, he began to notice that opportunities to be a different kind of actor sprang up. He finally had the lead role in a detective series, albeit as a serial killer. He still got the fame, money and affirmation he wanted and was considered important and influential in the acting community. He began to realize that it wasn't that he was denied an opportunity, he was just not noticing where better opportunities for him were.

'When the cicadas sing, rain is imminent' is an old cause-and-effect truism adopted by agrarian societies that sounds quite random. But observation shows that cicadas actually sing because of changes in weather, plant growth, temperature, humidity levels and their behaviour in the colder months. That is, on observation, we understand the whole cycle of changes a cicada goes through in order to 'predict rain'. Our intuition works in much the same way. We see the beginning and the end, but miss the whole cycle of influences that lie in between like a chain of cause and effect leading to an outcome.

When we use instruments of self-care, self-love, meditation, quietening down and stillness to raise the keenness of our observation, we become immediately more aware of what those influences are. We may make observations about aspects of our reactions that we have formerly missed, such as our own confidence levels and energy in different situations. We may work better when we feel safer, in non-toxic environments; we may be comfortable with members of the same gender; we may find obstacles or self-sabotage in ways that we are not even aware of when we are innately uncomfortable with where we are.

Inclusive awareness, a meditation:

Find a quiet spot in your home and sit comfortably on a chair or on the ground with a cushion. Close your eyes and just settle into the silence. Become aware of what is going on around you. Hear the sounds. They could be cars on the street, someone talking in the neighbourhood, clangs of vessels and the whirr of the fan. Identify yourself in the context of the sounds, where you are and where they are. Feel the sensations on your body. These could be heat or cold, or the breeze from the open window or fan hitting your skin. You could feel sweaty. Identify the parts of your body that give out specific sensations like an itch, aches, pains, a good feeling, comfort or relaxation. As you identify these, bring your attention to where your breath hits your philtrum, the area between the nose and the upper lip. Keep it focused there. Each time your mind wanders, bring it back to the breath. Observe what is happening to the sounds and sensations that you noticed earlier. Are they as loud? Have they receded into the background? The more your focus on your breath increases, the more these will fade from notice.

When we are able to see ourselves as standing at a confluence of influences, we are able to read our subconscious patterning and its expression better. We are more attuned with our environment. We become open to people and events, conversations and detours that enrich our life in ways that wouldn't on the straight and narrow. We become comfortable with the meandering journey. And the intuition becomes a razor-sharp instinct that helps us leap forward on a path that we intuitively know will work for us.

When the abruptness of change ceases to make sense, our intuition, gut instinct and synchronicity give us direction.

Take your power back.

In 2016, sociologist Warren TenHouten, at the University of California in Los Angeles, performed an experiment to test the feelings associated with powerlessness. After interviewing 564 Australian Aborigines and Euro-Australians, he concluded that powerlessness is based on four primary emotions (that are the same across cultures) – acceptance, expectation, sadness and fear. These come from objective powerlessness caused by inequality, inferiority, invisibility, economic distress and economic control. These act with six secondary emotions (our emotional reactions to primary emotions happen in ways that may be influenced by our upbringing or culture) – fatalism, pessimism, resignation, anxiety, submissiveness and shame. These become our subjective powerlessness.

If we have to cope with change and accept it, we are surrendering our feelings of power. How do we overcome that when moving ahead depends on our feeling empowered to do so?

Is there a way to accept change that doesn't feel like defeat, but instead like taking our power back?

The first step is refusing to be reactive to change. This disempowers the hold change has on us. We tell change, 'I am not your puppet.' We are not succumbing to our rage, anger, fear and disruption. We are navigating it in a systematic fashion that allows us to control the manner and magnitude of its effect on us, and how we express this effect. When we go through the Ocean pattern of coping, we are taking control of the aftermath of our change. In allowing the change to change us, we are calibrating our response to it.

The second stage is to delink effect from cause. That is, the goal is not the only possible outcome of the effort. When we do this, we reject the standardized patterning given to us. We already do this in some ways, but not others. For example, tradition states that girls who are disciplined, obedient and of a 'good moral character' get good husbands and have happy marriages and large families, and in this lies their happiness. We have begun to question, evaluate and reject this notion in favour of personal choice. We may choose not to marry, we may choose not to be 'good', we may choose not to have children. We may arrive at this shift in values involuntarily. Perhaps the man we dated and were loyal to cheated on us, leading us to re-evaluate the choices we abided by. We learned then that we were mistaken in linking the outcome to the effort. No one enjoys the feeling of the ground shifting from beneath our feet. It will take months and years to look back and see what has happened as an escape to a life better suited to us. In doing so we take our power back from the customs and traditions that pre-set the goals to the rewards on our behalf.

Anjali had been divorced and was being urged by her family to get married again. Reluctantly, she created profiles on various matrimonial sites and began to sift through matches. Finally, she found a good NRI match and the wedding was fixed. One of the conditions Anjali had laid down during her conversations with her fiancé was that since this was her second wedding, she would not ask her parents to pay for it; they would have to cover the expenses themselves. He had agreed to this in their initial meetings. As the wedding approached, however, he began to demand that her parents pay for the wedding. He wanted a more lavish venue and also started listing all the gifts he expected to receive from her. The day before the wedding, he called her and asked for a Cartier watch that would cost her ₹1.5 lakh. She asked him how he thought this was justified. His response was that she would be benefitting from his education so it was fair. Anjali disconnected the call, dialled her father and told him she would not be able to go through with the wedding. Her family was horrified, but Anjali knew she simply couldn't marry this man. They had been an engaged a year, the invitations had gone out, this would be a huge public embarrassment for the family. Some members of her family were initially quite vocal about their disapproval, but Anjali stuck to her gut. With one broken marriage already to her name, this just cast her in a worse light. She had to fight to hold her ground but realized that she simply could not surrender her power. Years later, the incident still rankled. The prospective groom found another woman willing to pay the dowry and was married by the end of the year. Anjali, scarred by the experience, put off marriage for another few years. With therapy and over time, she realized that as humiliating as the incident seemed then, it was not a relationship that would have worked for her long-term. She is now in a steady relationship that is more equitable and open, with a partner who is considerate of her need for independence. She feels nourished and understood. In hindsight, she is glad her second engagement didn't work out.

Who decides that a promotion is a reward for years of our hard work? Maybe for you it's the realization that the job you're in doesn't do it for you any more. Maybe it is time to gain new skills or find a way to make money off a hobby you love. The known goal, the stated outcome ceases to be the greatest reward we can possibly get, but instead acts like a ceiling that we will have to be satisfied with. It's one marshmallow.

However, we are the sky and we want the bounty of the seen and unseen world, not one marshmallow, or even two. If we are able to recalibrate all that is possible against what we imagine we deserve, we will find that we're actually selling ourselves short. Acceptance of change isn't acceptance of our powerlessness, it is a reclaiming of power no matter what the consequences.

The third stage is to feel this sense of entitlement. We're constantly telling ourselves to pace ourselves, think small, ask for little and be satisfied. We function from fear. Fly too high and we will also fail spectacularly we tell ourselves. This is because failing to reach that goal is so fraught. We have invested it with so much meaning that we have already decided our worthiness by our inability to meet the goal. So we function fearfully, in small ways, so that we fail in small ways. When we figuratively claim our expanded perspective, the world as ours, no punches held, we are opening our arms wide. We are casting off the sense of fear and trading it in for that of ownership. 'All of it is mine and I am entitled to my place under the sun.' We are rejecting all the voices of warning inside our heads and outside, the naysayers and their predictions if we fail to conform. The failure to reach a specific goal doesn't scare us so much any more. It's one of the milestones we wish we could reach, but now we have others; our bets have been hedged. We are imbued with a sense of fearlessness, confidence and ownership. Our failures are not our own, our victories are shared, we meet ourselves and others at a confluence of influences both conscious and subconscious, and we cease to measure ourselves by the limited maths of our lives.

Entitled to the earth, Qigong:

Assume the mountain pose as in Chapter Two, relax your shoulders, keep your feet grounded to the earth, shoulders relaxed. Breathe evenly and normally. Close your eyes for this exercise, keeping your gaze parallel to the ground. Come to complete stillness in this position. Feel the energy of the earth beneath your feet and the sky above your head. Feel the flow of energies on your right. Feel the flow of energies on your left. Become aware of the flow of energy in front of you and behind you. When you come to a complete stillness, you might feel a gentle vibration or pulsing, or the energy might be electrical or buzzing. You will know when you sense it. You will sense it when you are in complete harmony with it. Keep still until you feel yourself slipping into this complete oneness with your environment. When you feel it, gently raise your arms in front of you to shoulder level, as though you were loosely embracing a person. Keep your elbows soft, eyes closed, shoulders relaxed, and turn left from your hips. Use your best effort, without reluctance, tiredness or cynicism. Feel yourself stepping into the energy flow on your left. Repeat with the right side. Then come back to the centre, with arms still outstretched into the loose hug, and gently bring your arms towards your chest such that you are bringing the energy towards your heart. Send your arms out away from you again and bring them towards your chest again. Repeat a couple of times as though embracing the energy to yourself and feeling yourself as part of the energies outside you. The energy within your body should merge with the energy outside you seamlessly. Dissolve the boundaries around you as you expand yourself into the external energy. Feel yourself as one with the energy outside you. Observe that it is boundless, undefined in its scope, as limitless as the sky, expanding infinitely, receiving and giving symbiotically. As you dissolve yourself into this limitlessness, feel the energy in your body harmonize with the abundance of the sky.

8

How to Be the Sky

THE MEDITATIVE LIFE CAN FEEL LIKE A LUXURY. WE THINK of people who can conquer their emotions and master their reactions as renunciants. The rest of us have to live in this world. We have to work and cope and haul our families to better circumstances. How is all this philosophy going to work for us?

Yet, it is we, in all the trauma of our everyday lives, who need the insight the most. It's when you're being ripped off, taken for granted, toiling without thanks, and slammed on all sides by the pressures of existence that your buddha nature is called into service. The awakening inside you needs to hold the sky up when the storms of life rage through it.

Zen Master Eihei Dōgen noted in the Genjōkōan that 'the bird flies the sky and the sky flies the bird'. Both the bird and the sky retain their independence, but it is only because of each other, because of interconnection, that they come alive. Without the sky, the bird cannot fly. Through the bird, the sky comes to recognize its role. Within the moment of interconnection between these two lies the meaning of life. This is true for us too.

When we are the sky we become aware of our interconnection and how we impact others as well as how others impact us. None of us know our role or worth in isolation.

In stillness we come to a state of being that is aloof, distinct from the vicissitudes of life even as we experience them. It is not refusing to participate in life. To participate in life is to live with the ups and downs of it. To be still in the midst of all the chaos of life, gives us a valuable vantage point.

The eye of the hurricane is still. We have to move inwards to get shelter from the storm. Only in the midst of our chaos do we find our path.

Stillness isn't the lofty roof of the mind, where nothing untoward occurs. It is that across which all the variations of life play out. The sky sees howling winds, lashing lightning and throaty thunder. Twisters rip through parts of the world, devastating communities. The sky is the backdrop against which occasional but overwhelming cloudbursts that cause rivers to breach their banks occur. It looks on stoically as the sun blazes across the landscape below and parched beings suffer. The sky can be cruel and it can be kind. Yet, we do not attribute either quality to it. The sky is. Regardless of what expressions cross its face, what havoc the elements wreak on us, how much it hosts the instigating weather of our lives, we do not blame the sky.

And yet, what are we without it? It contains and circulates the oxygen we breathe, is the recycling facility for our water, drives the pollination of our world, encompasses mountains and reflects the depths. It protects, provokes, moves us to hunker down or sun ourselves. We look at the sky and say, 'Not today.' It drives our decisions to take a walk or travel, vacation, take a snow day or a rainy day, settle down with a cuppa or take a snooze. For all its macro expansiveness, it influences our micro decisions. Above all, we are powerless against it.

The Gauls believed the sky would fall on our heads as punishment and Chicken Licken went into a frenzy. We could shake fists at it, but it remains a steadfast and silent spectator as well as participant doing what it needs to do, regardless of our actions or opinions.

There is in fact no sky. It is just nothingness in increasing expansion. It extends boundlessly, capable of being and non-being at the same time. As it seems constant, it is changing.

When we identify with the sky, we extend ourselves in a spirit of compassion across all beings, animate and inanimate, visible and less visible to the human investigation. We become open and inclusive. The sky knows no man-made boundaries or distinctions. There is neither colour, caste, creed nor class; the sky is the same to everyone. Its cover stays over our heads whether we want it or not. It is offered whether you give thanks for it or not, desire it or not. Its compassion doesn't depend on your gratitude. It will nurture your weather and perform the same functions for you as it does for another. In this it is endlessly nurturing, sustaining and capable. It takes on responsibility and is unfailing.

The sky is open to possibility. What fails in its ambit fails and what is reborn is reborn. As the sky we are able to preside over what falls away from us with detachment. It witnesses the wrecks of ships, planes, civilizations and species that no one else can see. From that vantage point, we witness the landscape of our lives, strewn with our unique failings and fallouts, skeletons and fossils that we bury deep into the skin of our bodies and the topography of our minds. Entire forests grow over them as we push them down and move on, and fragments of our memories turn into emeralds and rubies, gold and diamonds with the passage of time. Someday, we will mine them for the wealth of experience they have to offer us.

We sustain multitudes. We are never constrained to the ground we cover in the immediate moment of our attention. We are wider than we are perceived to be, stretching into the horizon just when we think this is where our journey ends. There is more of ourselves to explore, if only we keep unfurling the depths within. To be the sky is to be constantly conscious of an unfolding vastness and yet to simultaneously preside over a seasonally flowering landscape. We consider the moment, but we act for eternity. We give ourselves the space to embrace our contradictions, neither lessened by what fails nor raised by what triumphs. We remain serene against the blame and gain of life; empires and monuments crumble beneath our expanse, and the details of mighty epochs of history now blur. Beings who believe themselves significant, play their roles and depart, and still the sky remains, unmoved. We extend ourselves to be used by those who would study us, relate to us and measure our qualities with the instruments of their benefit. We are, after all, here to be used.

We become expansive by lending ourselves to all of creation. We cannot be limited. Giving does not diminish us, neither does taking. The repository of our wealth derives from our ability to give, not from our need to take. Our ability to give arises from the awareness that anything that comes to us is given back in manifold ways, so it comes to us endlessly. It could be vapour, which is returned as rain; the value and culmination of journeys from one end to another. Our role is to bear witness to evolution, not to preserve the species or to hoard, and so we witness without intervening. Within the ambit of extensive space, wealth is an energy that is channelled and never clung to. We become a clear channel of passage that extends itself to the dispersal and dissemination of abundance. In this, the gaps and vacant spaces of our existence, we become valuable. If we were a thing, a block – complete, whole and occupied – we would be useful to no one. Because we both exist and do not, we lend ourselves to constant reinvention and application. We exist above, disaffected by all that happens below. We take life in our stride. In fact, the mutations of life become our entertainment and amusement. There is no pain that can be inflicted on us. As we become body-less and goalless, we become painless.

We cannot be diminished and we cannot be built up. We are. The sum of our parts is zero. We are both being and non-being. We are both doing and non-doing.

From the full, cleave the full, it is full.

From the empty, cleave the empty, it is empty.

This is how to be the sky.

9

The Travelling Cloud

The monsoon cloud shattered into fragments
with the thunder of a thousand storms.
Infant clouds
separated from each other and their mother,
pouring themselves out in sheets of abundant pain,
until Brother Wind took them by the hand
to far edges of a world that could be theirs.
Each cast its shadows above the valleys of orchards,
hovered over green fields of paddy, craving inundation,
chased the red-wattled lapwing and the green woodpecker
into the parched lands that heralded it like the hero
it did not know it was.
It turned cartwheels through a boundless playground.
Divided, each undiminished.
Multiplied, each a master of its domain.
Within each cloud a multitude
waiting to be broken from the bodies of their longing,
fractured into being again and again.
Above them, Mother Sky, all embracing, said nothing.

~

WHAT ARE THE WAYS IN WHICH WE CAN TRAVERSE THIS earth while coping with the suffering of change? The Tibetan Dzogchen tradition has a practice called sky gazing. It is considered the highest teaching. And yet, there is nothing for you to 'do' in it.

Sky gazing, a meditation:
Sit and gaze at the sky. As you breathe out, dissolve a little bit more into the sky.

The sky is the highest form of dissolution because you become the expanse. The meditation has an arriving, intensifying and dissolution phase, which is simply a letting go, allowing yourself to be dissolved into the ether. It is a state with no conceptual framework, when the mind ceases to see boundaries between oneself and another. This is why you pay no attention to breathing in; the identification as the distinct body ceases. What fills your lungs is no different than what nourishes your skin or sustains the plants and beasts. Arrive at the sky with the openness, without strain, without distinction, without rigidity. Now, unthink. As thoughts arise, release them entirely into the sky. The Dzogchen tradition is equated with the Sanskrit *mahasamadhi*, or complete union.

In all meditative practices, our instinct is to look for a special feeling, a unique experience because there is a whole industry that sells us meditation as though it is exotic. Is this going to feel like tripping out on weed? Will I not feel my body any more? Will I be able to feel my face? Meditation when it works for you is inclusive, remember? The sensation of awareness is not aimed at making us other than ourselves. It is an instrument to make us more real, more grounded and more ourselves than we knew possible. We need to try not to impose a sensation of what we imagine we ought to feel on our minds. That's the mind taking control of the experience again. We need to get to 'No Mind'. No Mind is where our thoughts and perceptions cease to impose on our reality.

No Mind does not mean we stop being who we are. It means we stop obstructing who we are.

In the stillness of seeing, we become more effective. We widen our vision and gain perspective of the vastness around us. As our practice widens us, we begin to reflect on reality far more completely and clearly. Of course, this is a process of expansion.

Consider seeing for a while in a world where our entire race is to be seen.

We seek to leave a mark, establish our legacy, and institutionalize and monetize ourselves. Tied into this is our sense of worth, self-esteem and validation. This impacts all our relationships. When we do not feel seen, the sense of lack permeates all our pursuits. That prestigious degree, the worthy job, the house on the hill, the legacy of industry, the progeny, the asset accumulation … all to say, 'We are here.' When in reality, all this does is keep us chasing the moving goalpost, never sufficient unto ourselves.

When we seek to see instead, we don't really need to do anything to establish our presence in the world. We simply have to find our stillness. Then we will begin to use the expansiveness we witness and that is reflected within us.

The philosophy arises from a core of consonance.

In qigong, a lot of physical and mental work involves embracing and allowing one's internal energy to become one with the external natural flow of energy in the world. We pulse to the more natural rhythm, where everything is not a chase. Where change is not the enemy. Where we rest in the constant becoming. We know this external energy of the universe exists, manifesting in the form of mass that Einstein equated to matter influenced by light. We invoke this unmanifest energy as *prana*, *qi*, or life force. When they say, 'come to alignment,' they mean harmonize with this life force and you will be in the rhythm of the world. Tap into it.

Qigong uses the five principles of direction, breath, posture, relaxation, and concentration through static and dynamic forms to achieve harmony with this energy. Alignment is not so much about physical sequencing. You don't physically jump into a river as it flows; you realize you don't need to. You are composed of the same essence as the river and if you tap into your inner stream, you will flow as one with it. The external expression is only a projection that is required when the internal is missing. All religious rites and rituals are intended to guide you towards identifying and discovering this unifying revelation. You are led to the external representation of the internal until you discover the stream for yourself. Qigong, yoga and meditation are about activating one's internal subtle force and bringing it into harmony with the external one.

Think of it like depressurizing an aeroplane cabin or coming up after a scuba dive. In order to come into balance with the external environment, two things have to happen: first, we have to witness the environment as it is, and second, we have to witness ourselves as we are. In depressurizing the cabin, we have to know the internal pressure and the discrepancy with the external pressure. We cannot come into harmony with an illusion or a delusion. We cannot assume. We witness these two aspects of the same pressure through our sensory inputs. We see, hear, feel, touch and assimilate things as they are. We do the same for ourselves as we are. Then we calibrate ourselves such that we dissolve the barriers between the two. This is the process of coming to equilibrium.

It is a gentle process – gradual, calming and filled with serenity. When we are equal to the external environment, there is nothing that we are in conflict with. Not death, decay, destruction or renewal; there is no grasping, collecting, hoarding or needing. Because we are in harmony with all of it, we need none of it. It is all ours by default. There is fluidity between us and the energy of the universe.

In yoga, we exert effort to revert to an original state of harmony that our body is capable of but perhaps does not have at this moment. We push the body into a physical alignment that will, in a state of perfect balance, click into a subtle alignment. The movement is from physical to subtle. Qigong calls upon us to use one's best effort to sense and project the subtle level, which then mobilizes the gross. Both perform the same function but approach it from different directions.

Strike a pose:

The cobra pose, or bhujangasana, *is a pose that earths you to the ground while sending your gaze skywards. The snake is a powerful symbol of rebirth and transformation in both Buddhism and Hinduism. A serpent is said to have sheltered the Buddha, as he meditated during a thunderstorm. The snake sheds its skin, transforming itself several times a year. During this process it becomes aggressive, disturbed by the process of its own change. The snake is, thus, both feared and revered. It is recognized as the harbinger of an essential but difficult change. The* kundalini, *the life force at the base of the spine is described as a coiled snake of energy. It is particularly targeted by this pose, which also opens the heart, sending a clear path of energy from the grounded feet to the sky via the fontanelle.*

Take a prone position on the floor and part your feet until they align with your hips.

Earth your toes to the ground. Plant your palms to the ground under your shoulders, fingers spread out, elbows pointing back towards your body. Raise your chest as you keep your pelvis on the ground. Push your shoulders back as you open out your heart to curve your spine inwards. Send your gaze skywards, tilting your head back. Breathe normally. The pose opens the heart chakra, activates the kundalini, grounds and earths the body and harmonizes one to the sky and ether.

To understand this alignment in terms of literary device, every time King Lear went ranting and rambling, Shakespeare ensured there was a storm outside to match his inner one. The heat of Romeo and Juliet's passion play out in the sweltering month of July. Prospero's howling winds match social disorder and being set adrift. And Rosalind's thawing winter turns to the spring of love.

Our alignment can be angry and passionate, or it can be peaceful. It depends on what we bring our attention to rest on. We choose the harmony we want to establish with the world because the world is a composite of both our internal forces and external ones. We are drawn to the manifestations of energy that we identify with. If it is storms we seek, storms we will get. If we align with anger, we will fill ourselves with it and resonate with it and it is what we will attract. Think of yourself as listening to the radio in the car as you drive. If your receiver is tuned to a particular frequency, you will only hear the stations that play on that frequency. If it's one that news channels broadcast on, you'll hear all the news channels. If it's one that all the jazz shows broadcast on, you'll hear all the jazz shows. To change what you hear, you will have to change the frequency you're listening on. Same with anger, hatred, jealousy, greed, and joy, happiness, generosity. The frequency you're receiving on is tuned in to what you'll hear. When our minds and emotions are filled with constant replays of a particular sentiment, that's what we're constantly tuning into outside us as well.

Sunil Alagappa grew his automobile business in Coimbatore in the hope that his son would take it over from him. His son, Suresh, studied engineering in California on a scholarship, but chose to stay behind and switch to IT, in which he felt the opportunities were better. He married a classmate, an American, and had children, which sealed the impossibility of his return. Father and son have had a strained relationship for the past few decades. While Suresh's mother visits him in the US, his father never has. Suresh worries that with his father's advancing age they may not have much time left and their rift may never heal. Suresh would like it if his father retired from his business by shutting it down, selling it or maybe handing it over to his cousin. At 76, Sunil still feels wounded by what he perceives as his son's betrayal towards his legacy. When his wife is away, often for six months at a stretch, Sunil stays behind, alone and feeling isolated from his family. 'Things are too far gone for me to change now, I am stuck in a rut of resentment,' he says. 'Whatever I tell myself, however logical it may seem, I still feel betrayed and let down by my son, my family, my life.'

Some psychologists think that positivity should not be forced. However, our negativity is not just forced, it is cultivated as a mindset. We focus on the bad or dissonant consciously, we berate ourselves for our failures, we are more willing to believe we deserve our punishments than our rewards, we scold ourselves more easily than we praise. We train our minds to locate the bad that has happened to us and convince ourselves it will repeat. We find ways to personalize our defeats. 'This was done to me,' we think. We validate the persecution, instead of taking cognizance of a combination of causes, conditions and effects. It feels like things have a single cause, but as we have seen earlier they don't always, it's often a combination of influences that creates outcomes that impact us. It may feel personal, but it isn't always. When we slow down and see, we observe that our own lives impact those of others in ways we are not always aware of. Miners in Brazil appealed to gold-loving Indians to stop buying what they termed 'blood gold' that came out of exploitative mines in the Amazon. They were grappling with mafias and murderous crime lords at every step of the way. An earring that brings us so much pleasure carries the pain of another. Even though we have not consciously done any harm in acquiring it, our lack of awareness in acquiring it implicates us in how the gold is extracted. This is why more and more of us are taking to sustainable living, and considering that our actions have wider implications than we comprehend. Even if we only understand suffering as being bodily and material, it is universal and interconnects us in insidious ways.

In this considered perspective, we depersonalize the negative and also the positive to see the good that has come to us unbidden.

Without looking outside of ourselves, our intentions, actions or conditions and peering through the windows of the world, we walk on with our personal rainclouds. We come to believe that when it rains, it rains exclusively on us. We nurture the sense that our suffering is special. We feel targeted and believe we will never quite outrun our misery. When we see suffering we see that it is universal. We see that the nature of our personal rainclouds is transitory. If these do not move with the wind, they rain themselves out. Even when we are caught in a squall, if we wait long enough, the downpour comes to an end. However, when we walk beneath our raincloud too long, we begin to nurture it. We cultivate it. We feed on the things that nourish and replenish it. We become attached to it. We begin to identify with it. We define ourselves by our misery. We have lived so long with what spiritualist Eckhart Tolle calls the 'pain body' that we mistake it to be ourselves. We introduce ourselves to others by its name. 'This is who I am,' we say. I have suffered in this way. I am my personal raincloud. It is easy to get caught up in this illusion that seems all too real.

The travelling cloud is itself driven to us by other factors of influence that we are not always conscious of. There are other winds that are caused by other actions, obstacles or the lack of them, direction, and purpose. We are not always privy to the wide scope of influences working in our favour or seemingly against us, but we find ourselves at a confluence not of our making, weathering a storm that we didn't expect.

The ideal is to find the balance between what we gain and what we lose. We are the participants in all kinds of energy. All energy mutates, passing from one phase into another, and we too will swing with the weather when we choose to identify with one form over another, positive or negative. We are constantly buffeted, raging and shifting from one to another.

To be the sky is to choose no weather. It is to come to alignment with the overarching energy and not its manifestations. To choose the end goal and not confuse it with the means to reach it. To values like alignment and equanimity, not jobs, designations and bank balances that allow us to walk that path. We witness the mutations, even partake in them but are not affected by them. We move out of the limitation our affliction has placed around us and step into a wider way of feeling and being.

The practice of oneness with the sky is a coming to harmony. And this is a conscious rewiring of our perspective. To this end, we use instruments like yoga, qigong, meditation or even music. However, these are much like drugs. They can heal when taken in the right dose and with regulation or targeted application, but unregulated, they can be harmful. They can cause dependencies and throw open a Pandora's box of emotion, thought and passion. They can begin to direct your thought process and play puppeteer to your emotional state, rather than remain the instruments of clarity. It is said that Raag Malkauns of the Bhairavi thaat has such an obsessive grip over listeners that even the most skilled masters will not play it without precaution and consideration because it can grip you and drive you to the depths of reclusiveness. A true master of kundalini energy will teach you to wield it only when he senses that you are ready for it. And yet there are kundalini yoga classes a dime a dozen. In the hands of a fool, sky gazing can turn from the highest meditative process to a wasted afternoon.

'Mindfulness' and 'wellness' have become buzzwords and are taught in decontextualized frameworks, becoming like popping painkillers to numb out our energy-sapping everyday routines. You will know a practice is working for you if it brings you into alignment with the natural rhythm and cycles of the world. This process will leave you feeling freed, connected and compassionate towards others.

If a practice is creating dependencies or side effects like uncontrolled outbursts of anger, too much anger, erratic sleep patterns, heightened emotions, it is either not the right practice for you or it is not being practised right. This applies to everything from a therapeutic intervention or a mindful one to addiction to physical exercise, binge eating or alcohol. Yoga practitioners are careful of *aparagriha*, a practice of non-attachment. See what your practice does for you. We do not all respond to the same practices the same way.

Whether your instrument is physical, spiritual or mental, it is only useful so far as it brings you to alignment. These are all travelling clouds across the face of our individual skies. Don't mistake the clouds for the sky. As the Buddha said, 'Don't mistake the finger pointing at the moon for the moon.'

How do we make change work in our favour instead of being subject and victim to its mutations? Taking to the Ocean pattern of acceptance allows us to be in the moment, grieve, realign, get into the right frame of mind and deal with the suffering of change. But it is in becoming the sky that we are able to become elementally bigger than the challenges that we face. As lofty and metaphysical as this feels, by repeatedly touching earth and seeing sky, like in the Bhujangasana, we are called upon to implement it in our lives. Think of it as Michelle

Obama's statement, 'When they go low, we go high.' When we lift ourselves above the small stuff, towards boundlessness and infinitude, we find ourselves disaffected by the changes that occur. And we can use the changes thrust on us to our advantage.

However, if I am the sky, why should I do anything? Do I just sit at my window and gaze at the sky all day? Who pays my bills? Who feeds my children? Why act at all, if we have found our stillness anyway? The reason is because even if we have, others haven't. Besides, the former is also debatable. We may snatch glimpses of the stillness from time to time, but only a few of us are completely psychologically resolved or spiritually awakened. We are pretty much all works in progress. This is the essence of the bodhisattva way. If we find ourselves awakened, we need to awaken others. Because suffering of change is universal, we are all mired in it and we are interdependent, therefore, none of us rise alone. The unawakened state of others also impacts us. The capacity for change is individual, but it is also social, political and global. So, the challenge to change is best posed by those who push, help or enable others to radical empathetic change at considerable cost to themselves.

Salil Tripathi, journalist, author and activist, has spent years devoting himself to humanitarian causes. His interest in human rights began as a teenager in school when India underwent Emergency in the mid-1970s, his volunteer work with the newly-minted PUCL, campaigning for the Janta Party, and later with running the campus Amnesty group as a student at Dartmouth College. A key aspect of his voluntary work as chair of Writers in Prison Committee at PEN International includes mobilising help for those writers, journalists, and others who face threats by authoritarian governments and one of the key questions is, given the risk, backlash and threat to himself, how does one keep pushing for change, though it may be personally hard to do so.

'Pragmatism is very important and we have to keep re-interpreting the past but in order to do so we need to have a very strong core of values that guide our thinking and that means treating others the way one wants to be treated,' Salil points out. A solid core of compassion leads the way in which we look at and cope with change. 'Pure empathy often helps to drive the efforts of those who do humanitarian work. When I find someone who wants to write but cannot, I put myself in their position and ask what I would have wanted others to do for me when I can't write – and that gives me a clue about what I should do. It means listening to the one who one wants to help. That's how I understand empathy, and it also means not imposing myself.' Sometimes this also means campaigning for the freedoms of people whose ideas he later has to come to disagree with, like with Aung Sang Suu Kyi. When the change you expect is not the change that you get or worked for, how do you keep at it?

'Don't put anybody on a pedestal as far as possible. In my life I have met four people – the Dalai Lama, Nelson Mandela, Vaclav Havel, and Aung San Suu Kyi – that someone from a distance would have admired. I thought that meeting them was my nirvana, but they each had their weaknesses. For me, Havel is taller than the others, except that he too mistakenly, according to many, supported the war in Iraq. Everybody is flawed and if you put anyone on a pedestal, they will fall. Even M.K. Gandhi is seen differently by many, but as Orwell said when he died, "how clean a smell he has managed to leave behind!". Human rights defenders are special because what we like about them is that they are victims, and are suffering and steadfast, which to some feels like they're being stubborn. If they are not stubborn they will be like you and me, who might be vulnerable and crumble under torture. So I admire those who can

burn themselves at the stake like Joan of Arc. But that stubbornness also sometimes makes them unpleasant and contrarian for the sake of being so.'

The same qualities that allow us to lead others out of difficult times and into progressive change can also become our blind spots, Salil notes. 'One should not assume victims cannot turn into perpetrators themselves. There are many who have experienced horror stories of facing Partition, or witnessing their own sisters being raped or loved ones killed in a genocide, but who end up with zero empathy for others, since they can't escape their victimhood and confuse justice with revenge. So, it doesn't always translate. The sensible thing to do with all of that is to simply put yourself in other people's shoes. When you do that you will see that each grievance is special, but if you look at the entire world solely through that grievance you will miss out a lot.' This plays out in debates all through our social and political worlds, from the rights of transwomen to those who have lived through genocide and their need for retaliation. 'Sometimes, it becomes a war between two vulnerabilities,' Salil says. 'There is no formula for navigating these dilemmas, you have to keep pushing for the change that you think is right, to displace the outdated and oppressive and call upon your core of values to keep at it. What you do is you hope that the reasonableness of your argument will prevail. Just because something is wrong does not give the sanction for its counter to be right. We don't need to set our benchmarks low and should avoid Manichean responses.' Salil says it's impossible to know which aspect of our work creates momentum, but everyone arrives at their own tipping point by which they begin to see differently, and it is our role to keep contributing to that through empathy, compassion, and the outward gaze.

In the Zen tradition, the absolute and relative are not contradictions. They coexist. We are being and non-being. We do and we don't. A lot of human progress has come from doing. We take a higher perspective on life, but we also know that we are part of humanity. If we take human suffering as a given, what is the need for compassion, medical interventions, social justice or equality? Through our clarity, we have become responsive. We act as the moment demands it, knowing all the while there is an absolute. Our giving a man water may not mean he will never be thirsty again, but for the immediate moment, we have served him with compassion, a cause that will create a further effect in him. Perhaps it's a pay-it-forward that will lead him to a path of compassion and less suffering. We consider what the moment needs, knowing we don't control the outcomes, but collectively, we can try to influence it. When we are hungry we still eat. Though if we are the sky, ideally we should feel no such thing as hunger. Being disaffected is not that we witness the horrors of the world, unmoved. We don't turn our face away from what is unfolding before our eyes. We move outside our limited framework to use our suffering from change to impact others, in whatever small ways we can.

Sanjai, 44, worked in a media organization and was flustered when the pandemic hit. He was energetic, gregarious, outgoing and highly sociable – traits that helped him in his performance in a high-tension business service where you outpace your rivals by breaking stories with a lead time as short as six seconds. He was terrified that the lockdown would bring him a slowing down of pace that meant he would 'start sinking into a black void'. Then, a friend needed help to travel to Kerala to help his father and Sanjai couldn't turn him down. Entrusting his deadlines to a dongle, a not too speedy internet connection, was Sanjai's first risk. But he took the opportunity, travelled with his friend and returned to his own family home in Kerala. In the evenings, he worked at his farm and paddy field. He started a WhatsApp study group for kids that took off, 'like a silent volcano'. As days stretched to months his perspective began to change. He began to help his parents get their lives in order, then turned to helping patients infected with Covid-19 to get hospital beds or communicate with their families. He began to enjoy 'being the bridge,' he says, and participating in the lives of others in this way. He noticed that while earlier his worries were deeply personal, now he had expanded the circle and in the midst of the pandemic he could find a sense of purpose. He started feeling 'more human'. He began to realize that when we do what we can to widen our circle, our perspective changes.

What allowed him to make the shift from a mindset of despair to that of expansion? 'It helped to know that others were in a similar boat. It wasn't just me. It was my work rivals, the whole country, the whole nation. That allowed me to stop feeling persecuted and freed up my mind space to start thinking about others,' he says.

A couple of ground rules worked for him. 'First, don't think too much. When you know that nobody knows what's happening, nobody has control, not the prime minister, not the scientists, no one knows if we need herd immunity, or a vaccine, when everyone's floundering, you learn that you can let go too. You're not going to find answers that nobody else has. Second, you have a choice to grope in the dark and flounder along with everyone else, or move steadily along. You can't drive at 100 miles per hour, but you can drive at 5 miles per hour and ensure you don't bump into anyone else. Third, is the slowing down of the pace. When you slow down, you begin to see the road ahead of you more clearly. When you get that clarity, you now see that there is no way but to fight back. And when you fight back, you gather people with you. You don't fight back alone. You take the power of the collective. This becomes the structure for your new way of approaching life.' Sanjai has since returned to Mumbai, but he says the lessons have stayed with him.

When we slow down, we see what is needed in the moment. We are best equipped to respond to the needs of the moment when we no longer identify with the high-pressure occurrence. This depersonalizes the event and removes our emotions from the equation. The unfolding event has become a travelling cloud across our sky and we can offer interventions that range from putting up an umbrella, building shelters and pulling people out of the flood waters, but we see it now for what it is, a passing storm and little more. We cease to define ourselves by the weather. We see now with clarity that we were fine before and that we will be fine after. Our worry is no longer so much for ourselves. As our attention gets freed up from constant concern with our state of mind or being, we are able to divert it to others. This is how many ordinary people are able to rise to extraordinary circumstances and help those around them who are struggling.

In order to be non-reactive, we have to start becoming mindful about the impact of our actions, knowing they have the capacity to impact another's well-being one way or another.

How do we respond to change that is disruptive without being disruptive ourselves? Disruption is a cause, and instead of a reaction, when we offer a pause, consideration and a response, we disrupt the cycle of reactivity. We transform the transformation. We do not offer another disruption in reaction. We do not react with emotionality, whether that is anger or elation. We respond as appropriate to the moment. If someone we love has passed, we are able to pull ourselves from the grief and see to what those who leave behind need from us. We step in. We act. We pull ourselves back from spending too much of our emotion into the passing, and we reserve a little for the phase of life that is the aftermath. A woman who has lost a partner may need to pull herself together to manage finances, assets, business, work, income, children and other pragmatic routines of life. When we become overwhelmed by grief we either stop functioning, or function by repressing our pain in such a way that is erupts in our health and mental well-being. If we are able to acknowledge our pain, grieve, release, realign and accept, we will be able to move forward and do the things that we need to do, for ourselves as well as others. We have some of ourselves left to spark the moving on.

Anitya, Impermanence, may be a metaphysical truth, but it is a lived reality. We can only cope with it with utter pragmatism. The high philosophy of the skyward gaze must touch the ground through our toes. To cope with change is to smoothen our passage through life.

When we are able to conserve our mental, physical and spiritual resources in this way, we are able to do justice to what is, what was and what will be. Sometimes we spend so much of grief on the pain of the moment that we deplete ourselves, leaving us with very little energy for rebuilding. When we have to move on because circumstances demand that we do, we carry the guilt of not having grieved enough, we feel like moving on becomes a betrayal of the person who has passed. We forget that all phases, no matter how severe and debilitating, will pass. When we have framed change as the enemy, have taken its confrontation personally, held on to resentment, we are spending all our energy on the collapse. It's what we do when we exit a relationship and spend all our time thinking about our ex instead of putting our energy into recovering from the break-up and moving on. When you change jobs, you don't keep working at your old role, you move into the challenges of the new one, even if you have a learning curve. In our pain of change, we forget that what we have lost to change is less important than what we will gain by change, and we don't reserve our emotional, mental, physical and spiritual strength to navigate it.

When Naseeruddin Hodja arrived for a lecture he was supposed to deliver in another town, he was taken aback to find only one man in the audience. So he asked him if he should start the lecture or let him leave. The attendee replied, 'Sir I am just a humble farmer, but when I go to the barn at lunchtime and find only one cow there, I feed it regardless.' Pleased with the response, Naseeruddin Hodja commenced his lecture. He spoke for three hours. When he had finished, he asked the farmer what he thought. The attendee replied, 'Sir I am just a humble farmer, but when I go to the barn at lunchtime and find only one cow there, I don't feed it the stock of fodder that the entire herd would consume.'

When we step back and be the backdrop against which we allow life's storms and sunshine to play their patterns, we are also able to intervene only when and as necessary.

If you are a mother, you may watch your child play but intervene strategically to ensure they are safe and healthy. The rest is a mess you know you can clean up. As one of my Vipassana meditation teachers, Mr Daniel Mayer, said to me, 'Be as a mother to yourself, help yourself along.' Qigong asks us to bring our 'best effort' but also bring only as much of the effort as is required. Don't bring a canon to a knife fight. The intensity of our grief for what we have left behind is dictated by whether we are the cloud or the sky.

When we are the sky, the loss of the cloud is incidental. We are able to pass through the world without really leaving a trace.

But wait a minute, you may think you want to leave a trace, don't you?

Sure, we don't all want to be Ozymandiases, but we want to leave our mark on the world. We want to contribute in a way that is meaningful. We want to write a book, we want to create an art work, design a building, a cityscape, put in place an economic policy or plan, or create a medical intervention that will confer some betterment on the lives of others. We want to leave the world a better place, don't we? We want to look back at the end of our lives and feel that we mattered. So how do we travel the world without leaving a trace and still achieve that?

When we create without an attachment to who gets the credit, without an eye on the award and reward, when we are able to contribute without seeking to own the contribution and controlling the outcome, we are able to make a difference.

This becomes easier to do when we see the world as one. Not in terms of platitudes, but in terms of seeing our own boundless energy resonant in others and theirs in us. When we dissolve these boundaries between ourselves and the world, when we recognize that we breathe the same air, we sustain ourselves in the same way, the same life force that pushes the plant out of the seed is in our children and those of others, we become quite detached from ideas such as credit and ownership. This allows us to release our goals and ambitions and moves us towards experiencing the world through authentic connectedness. We also recognize ourselves as incidental to the performance theatre of energy. Energy that has manifested through us, thanks to a certain confluence of thoughts, ideas, feelings and actions, could just as well have manifested through another. We don't become special in our doing, we remain ordinary. And in our ordinariness, we find ourselves connected and nurtured even as we connect and nurture others.

When we act from this space of undifferentiated interconnectedness, we harmonize with the energy of the world.

This is how to navigate our change with the equanimity and expansiveness of the sky.

FIRE

Magga, the Way Out

10

Burnout

From the wood, a spark
From a spark, the flame
From a flame, fire
From a fire, the blaze
From a blaze, energy
From the energy, creation
From a creation, the forging
From the forging, an object
From the object, decay
From the decay, deconstruction
From the deconstruction, death
From the death, elements
From the elements, sediment
From the sediment, the earth
From the earth, growth
From the growth, the urge for life
From the urge for life, a seed
From the seed, a tree
From the tree, wood
From the wood, a spark.

~

IF THE THINGS THAT PROVOKE US ARE TRANSIENT, AND SO are our responses, how does anything changing matter? We become free to set our own intentions, act on them and hope for the outcomes we seek.

In the Adittapryaya Sutra, which is the Buddha's Fire Sermon, he says, 'Monks, the All is aflame. What All is aflame? The eye is aflame. Forms are aflame. Consciousness at the eye is aflame. Contact at the eye is aflame. And whatever there is that arises in dependence on contact at the eye – experienced as pleasure, pain or neither pleasure nor pain – that too is aflame. Aflame with what? Aflame with the fire of passion, the fire of aversion, the fire of delusion. Aflame, I tell you, with birth, aging and death, with sorrows, lamentations, pains, distresses and despairs.'

Nibbana, the Pali word for nirvana, means extinguishing of the flame, and this has many interpretations.

Everything we see, hear, taste, touch, smell or think, everything that comes to us through our sensory inputs feeds our passions. Our passions are what incite clinginess, attachment, aversion and sorrow through sensuality, views, opinions, precepts, practices, doctrines and ideology. We can't stop their onslaught. We can't stop the breeze from hitting us any more than we can halt the jostle of the crowd in a marketplace. And if we did find a way, it would seem like we have ceased living. What we want is a better way to live, not quitting life as we know it.

If we cannot stop what comes at us, it is out of our control, we can focus on what is within our control: our reaction to it all.

Magga is the way out. This is The Buddha's Fourth Noble Truth. The gate of Magga is in awakening. We allow ourselves to be reborn when we burnout.

When a fire is extinguished, it turns to ember and ash, elemental and basic. Ash cannot revert to fire. Fire cannot revert to wood. We do not un-die. We move forward to be recycled into the stuff of life. All religion, whether using dust or sacred ash, honours this elemental return to a primal state. We don't die to die out, we die to be reborn. We die in the way that winter makes way for spring. It doesn't turn into spring, spring is a renewal all of its own. Nor is winter entirely gone. We recognize that it surrenders to its elemental nature to return in another form at another time.

We all spring anew in this way.

Burning out is coming to Sunyata, which is not so much nothingness, its most common translation, as it is a constant changingness. Things move so rapidly that nothing is permanent. Psychologically, however, the lens on the burnout sees it as an illness. In 1974, psychologist Herbert Freudenberger discovered that burnout was a thing and that it emanated from emotional exhaustion, cynicism and low self-esteem. These three aspects formed the basis for the Maslach Burnout Inventory, a standardized test to quantify burnout in individuals in various settings. We use it to help people avoid inflicting emotional and mental self-harm upon themselves as they go about their jobs. The consequences of burnout have been particularly real for doctors and healthcare workers during the Covid-19 pandemic.

Should we embrace burnout?

When we identify a cause of burnout in a biomedical model, we're seeking a way to fix it and carry on doing what we've always been doing. When we find we have a fever, we want a solution – a tablet, an injection or a period of rest – so that we can recover and proceed with our lives. We use medical solutions to return us to the way we were before we experienced the fever. So we develop 'coping strategies'.

That's also why we're all looking for coping strategies to deal with change.

There aren't any. There are only coping strategies to keep you going until you realize that you will need to accept the change. That change is inevitable. 'Do not push the river, it flows by itself,' said Fritz Perls, the founder of Gestalt therapy, an integrative mind-body-spirit therapeutic theory. When we seek to 'cure' burnout, we are ignoring what the burnout is telling us. We are not paying attention to its lesson. You wouldn't just drive on in a car that had a beeping indicator on the dashboard. You would surmise that it could crash or stop. You wouldn't ask a mechanic to just stop the beeping so that you could get on your way. You would want to know the cause of the beeping, investigate the source, and resolve it. You cannot drive on in the vehicle as before. You would want to know its processes have been tinkered with and corrected before you can proceed. This is what change does for us. It points our attention towards the beeping and asks us to investigate. This is when you decide you won't get back in the vehicle and ignore the beeping.

That the only way to get past the pain is to go through it.

The only way to get past change is to undergo it.

Gestalt therapy functions on three zones of awareness. Awareness in this context is simply being in touch with your natural states, ranging from asleep to completely energized. Our three zones are the outer zone, the middle zone and the inner zone. The inner zone is the inner physical world, your heartbeat, your pulse rate, the tension in your muscles, your breathing. The middle zone is our thinking, our emotions, our perception and our memories. The outer zone is how we connect with the world around us, comprising our speech, behaviour and actions. We often get stuck on one or another of these zones.

Step into the awareness continuum:
Ask a trusted friend to sit with you. As you tell them how you are coping or not coping with the change that has befallen you, consider your three zones. Notice your inner zone, your physical manifestations as you are speaking, changes in pulse rate, any quickening of the heartbeat, shortening or quickening of breathing. Notice your middle zone, what you are thinking and feeling, memories that come up that you are not really communicating. What difficult memories surge back to you? What is your perception of the situation and what emotion does that bring up in you? Name your emotions. Then observe your outer zone, the manner in which you are conveying your story, your words, your gestures, your actions. Are they in alignment with the inner and middle zones? Or are they dissonant? For instance, do you think you are calm but are you in fact pacing or gesticulating anxiously? Do the outer and inner zones match? Is the frustration manifesting equally in your heart rate or breath as in your speech and gestures? Or is your outer zone more subdued? Focus on staying in the moment, widening your awareness of your experience, paying attention to what you are avoiding expressing or thinking.

When you've done this a couple of times, go through a cycle of experience. Watch a sensation, name it and observe how it impacts your inner zone. Think of what thoughts and emotions it provokes and name them. Be aware of the point at which you decide to respond, watch how this manifests in speech, gesture and expression, and how you come to express the original sensation. The cycle is sensation, recognition, mobilization, action, contact, satisfaction and withdrawal.

When you complete the whole life cycle, you will come to the cessation of the original sensation. Just stay there. Be. This is the fertile void. From awareness of this, all renewal springs.

People experience burnout in their jobs which is contextual, located largely within the economic cycle. Burnout is a threat not just to people and their mental health, but to the myth of constant creation, continuum and permanence that needs workers to set aside their well-being in order to keep the profit machinery turning. It interrupts the notion that we can be endlessly productive. Burnout within this taxing, imposed cycle is unexpected and exhausting. Burnout that occurs in the elemental structure is natural, inevitable and replenishing.

Everything in the elemental cycle burns itself out in order to create anew. A living tree turns its falling leaves to mulch at its feet from where it will return to replenish the very earth that nourishes its roots. This is an organic decay, a natural completion of purpose that doesn't seem to be built into the economic cycle that demands we continue unabated. All things decline. All beings run out of a capacity to cope with challenges, even ones they used to be able to cope with before. It's not a human failing to be unable to cope. It is a failing of the system that forces us to cope. Burnout is non-threatening in the natural space. And it doesn't need fixing; it needs acceptance. We will outgrow our former selves in the way that a tree sheds leaves.

Modern life demands we find ways to remain in a constant and steady pace of creation that is unnatural.

When we gain the adeptness to observe the cycle of experience in its entirety, we will note how naturally we pass from stage to stage, the previous one dying out in order for the next to arise. Sometimes when we're very angry, we feel a tremor, a physical burning in the pit of the belly, and when we finish screaming at the object of our ire, the sensation passes away. We may weep with relief, the body releasing the immense pressure it took on to sustain the whole cycle.

There is no wrong or right in the cycle. There are no actions we must not undertake or sensations we should not feel. The more intimately we observe ourselves the more we become aware of our patterns. Let's say we become really angry at a partner. With increased self-observation, we will be able to observe the onset of tightness and the clenching in the jaw, or the abdominal muscles that lets us know we are getting really angry. When we have become accustomed to mapping our patterns in this way, the tell-tale signs of emotion that the body puts out, we will be able to intervene. We can find a way to distract ourselves and prevent the emotion from bursting out. We may go watch a show or do some gardening until we calm down and can return to the conversation. We use this self-knowledge to control what formerly felt like an impulse. We achieve a sort of mastery in putting a pause to our reactions. We are able to cut the cycle short.

This is how a continuum of awareness allows us to take control of the change.

In the Lotus Sutra, the Buddha explains that we are living in a house that is on fire. When we grasp for permanence, we are clutching at the shadows cast by the flames. As the flames dance, we undergo suffering in our grasping. With awareness we recognize the flames for what they are and exit the house, saving ourselves from this pursuit.

In psychology, this is mirrored by Arnold Beisser's Paradoxical Theory of Change. It states that, 'change occurs when one becomes what he is, not when one becomes what he is not.'

Psychology, like the philosophy of the Buddha, believes that every individual has the resources for self-awareness within themselves. Change in Beisser's context is therapeutic change, the process of healing and self-discovery. It is a forward movement towards self-acceptance, harmony and alignment – the point of equilibrium when we are able to cope with the changes that come our way. Most of our trips into therapy also arise from being unable to cope with the change that has either occurred in the past, is ongoing or that we fear in the future. This becomes the source of our anxiety. Alignment would then mean remaining unfearful of the impending change. All our resistance to change takes us further away from who we are. This is why we need to hang on to the idea of creative indifference. In both psychology and the teachings of the Buddha, we come to realize that we cannot fixate on a goal but acquire the inherent dynamism to be fluid on the path. Even the pursuit of nirvana detracts from the journey. You follow your path to where it leads and crave no particular end, open to all outcomes. This is a key lesson that eases the way we take to life. When we are creatively indifferent, we embrace who we are without directing ourselves to a predetermined idea of who we think we should be. Transformation comes, according to Beisser, when we give up the idea of who we ought to be and become fully, in the moment, just who we are. Know who you are. Be aware of your zones. And just be.

When we are who we are, and are secure in that knowledge, change loses its power over us. It becomes an organic process in step with the rhythm of the world. As the seed becomes the plant, the plant sprouts the flower, and then the flower becomes the seed again. The seed is then carried by winds, animals and other means of dissemination and finds its way into the world where it perpetuates the cycle again. It is an organic process. We can't force it any more than we can peel back the petals of a flower to make it bloom. We are a part of this cycle and our change, impatient or reluctant as we may be for it, too blooms through this rhythm. As we impact the seed by consuming it, something else impacts us. There is no part of this cycle that we enter into in isolation. Hence, there is no part of this cycle that we exit on our own either. We play our part in it with awareness and participation that comes from compassion, from seeing our own role and those of others.

This is how we take responsibility for our lives.

Having done so, we walk through the tough changes with clarity. It is not that the hard parts disappear. They are still there, but because we see how they happen and how we hold ourselves back, they just become easier to navigate. We take the tough calls. We make the difficult decisions.

Let us be conscious of the fact that our journey of embracing change, as difficult as it is for us, can be difficult for others around us too. Just because we have come to terms with change in our lives doesn't mean those around us have. They might still be struggling for answers and reasons. And they in turn may, unintentionally, make it difficult for us to undertake our own journey.

Responses to change may emerge as anger and resentment. We may be asked: 'How are you able to move on so quickly? It means you never really loved them.' Or it may emerge as disbelief: 'I don't trust the changes you've made.' It can be hard when you've also borne the brunt of your change and have struggled to accept it. Think of addicts who have come through recovery only to be told their partner or family doesn't believe they'll remain sober, or a person who has harmed others, served his time and returns to tell others he has changed.

The story of Vajrayana master Milarepa's revenge is a great example of this.

Jetsun Milarepa was born into a wealthy family. But after his father's death, his uncle and aunt forced Milarepa and his mother to become the help in their own home. His mother urged him to study black magic to exact revenge. He did so and became a master in the form. After he exacted revenge on his uncle and aunt, he was struck with remorse and found himself a true teacher in Marpa, who gave him a task to purify the negative karma he had earned through his vengeance. He had to build, destroy and rebuild a stack of stone towers repeatedly. Milarepa did this day in, day out, nearly pushed to the brink of despair before Marpa would take him on as his disciple. Eventually, Milarepa became a cotton-clad yogi in the Himalayas, a teacher, and composed The Hundred Thousand Songs, *a collection of poems that are passed down to this day.*

Though the story of Milarepa has been interpreted at various mystical and philosophical levels, its essence rests in the belief that we are immensely capable of change, no matter what we have done or been through. That everything can and does change is fundamental to both, psychology and the teachings of the Buddha.

In fact it is in change and through change that we transform into ourselves.

This is how we move from change as a burden to change as healing.

Why is it inevitable that we leave people behind when we change?

Because our change is not their change, and their change is not ours. Because our change does not change the world. It only changes our perspective of the world. Because as much as we are interdependent, we each walk alone. Our journey or path does not belong to anyone else. No one, as Neo said, can tell you what the Matrix is. You have to discover it for yourself and when you do, you will need the willingness and openness to walk the path it directs you along. Our paths are our own.

Changes in our learning and perspective are only a part of our process. One insight doesn't directly transform years of cultivated habit. We all know how hard it is to change an eating habit or a smoking habit even when we know they are harmful. Knowing is not doing, doing is not living. So long as our change remains unidimensional, its impact remains within our limited ambit.

It is only when our changed perspective permeates our body, mind and spirit, becomes expressed through our thoughts, words and actions, that we begin to impact the environment around us. Then we are able to take the change we have arrived at involuntarily, we are able to allow the change to change us, we are able to transform our own transformation and step forward into an authentic sense of self, which further helps us impact others. This is how to merge with our change.

II

How to Be Fire

WE ARE AT OUR WORST WHEN OUR PASSIONS ARE AT THEIR best.

Everything in and around us is heightened. When the fires of our sensory inputs are blazing away, they consume everything that comes into contact with them. This could range from the food we eat to the news we greedily imbibe from multiple sources; we have no filters. We walk around with too much. Too much food, too much want, too much need, too much thought, too much sight, too much smell. As a result we are, throughout our days, a dancing wildfire.

The 2020 wildfires of Australia burned about 27.2 million acres of forest, affecting human settlements and species populations for years to come. There have been an average of 50,000 distinct wildfires in the US over the last couple of years, destroying around 6 million acres of forest a year. Fires are all-consuming when they get going, feeding off the inputs in their path until they blaze themselves out. We sleep, wake, think, feel and act with fires blazing inside us. We all know what it is to want, need, feel deeply or seek passionately. We have come to nurture the flames of our longings. We romanticize the ache for a lover, an ambition, fame, money or status symbols. We align sharply with one ideology or another, defending our positions as though our lives depend upon it. We condemn others with vehemence, some of us even making threats and going through with them. We will fight and die for specific principles because they seem so much bigger than us, and we believe we will create continuum by committing our mortal acts and words to the immortality of the ideal.

All for that which does not last or cannot last, will not, despite your best effort.

Why then are we walking around with blazing fires like these inside us?

There are two ways in which we can deal with this burden. Firstly, we recognize that our goals are impermanent in themselves. Secondly, we re-evaluate the degree of our attachment to the goal.

A thinker we idolize today might prove to be disappointing tomorrow. Or on the contrary, a text we derive our values from might be in sore need of updating, stubbornly refusing to change. When we keep the transitory nature of what we admire or aspire to in mind, we proceed with caution. We curb the passion with which we process inputs. We put a pause to how passionate we become about things. We might become less vehement about professing an ideology, we might think more about the parts of it that we can be on board with. We move from the assumption of 'all things being constant' to 'all things are liable to change'. The inevitability of change brings us dispassion and moves us to a middle path. We are no longer in the throes of self-assuredness, betting our lives and those of others on the mutable.

When we stop seeing change as the enemy, it ceases to have power over us.

When we stop seeing our passions as our masters, we limit their control over us.

Both of these simultaneously reduces the impact change has on our lives.

The Buddha insisted that his students question their masters repeatedly and look not to emulate them but their best qualities instead. When we are dispassionate about what we believe in, we are able to take the best and release the worst of them.

When we befriend change but do not turn down the flames of our passion, they still consume all our energy and time. We are still constantly provoked. All it takes is a Tweet from someone we don't even know to ruin our day. Because in a landscape on fire, every dry twig is kindling. Everything we consume in our day-to-day lives – a news telecast, a movie, a song, food, conversations – contributes to our state of mind, body and spirit. This keeps the flames going.

The basic firefighting technique is to cut off the source of oxygen.

What does this mean for us? We are not yogis or sadhus, monks or masters, seers or sages. We are ordinary people trying to make it through really difficult periods without being obstructed or caught off guard every time we make a plan. Logic says that if I set an intention towards a goal, work hard, do what's right ethically and morally, my path should be a straight line from point A to B. However, we now know this is rarely so because of various factors, ranging from the strength of the intention to the conditions on the way, how others impact us, and the validity of the goal from our limited perspectives. We all want to enjoy a nice meal, have a drink with friends, travel, save money, get opportunities to showcase our talents, have healthy relationships and lead a fulfilling and safe life. There isn't anyone who doesn't want a life filled with these goals with a few add-ons.

Not getting to reach our goals is the source of our dissatisfaction, but that obstruction is also what sets us on the path of change. The process of understanding why we are on that detour is the path of awakening. Being okay with what we don't get is the path of our stillness. Regulating what in us pursues them is the path of springing anew.

Fire is a powerful tool of self-awareness. While the Buddha used it to describe the fire we burn with, he also used it to describe the illumination of the highest mind, the *bodhicitta*. Wildfire is destructive, but a fire under control is the light of wisdom. Fire is also the *prana* or *qi*, the life force that emanates as breath. It is what keeps us alive.

Extinguishing this fire may be the highest ideal, the liberation from the cycles of life and death, the aches of samsara, or worldly existence, the constant ups and downs, but as we turn with the wheel of existence, we need the fire within us to drive us to perform.

A house on fire leaves us on the street, but the fire in the kitchen stove sustains us. When we control the fires blazing within us, we use their blaze to sustain ourselves. The fires of sight, sound, feeling, word, thought and deed are the instruments of our change.

When we become mindful of the fires within us and the transience around us, we will consider deeply what we are allowing to feed us. When we become deeply aware of the impact these inputs have on our output, observe how they derail us, how they stir thoughts and dissatisfactions, we will minimize the impact upon ourselves. We develop the power to discern, which sows the seeds of wisdom. True discerning is self-protective and selective. It nurtures the calming of passions, it chooses what we respond to and when. It prioritizes our engagements. It conserves our energy. The process of arriving at discerning declutters our mind and removes the objects or people who contribute to the inflamed state, knowingly or unknowingly. This is also another reason why it is natural to find friends and family, or acquaintances, old hobbies and interests fall away at this time. As we become more aligned with our energy, we begin to streamline what has the power to influence us. This is not a cutting off that emerges from fear or exasperation with the world. That would be rejection, and as we know rejection is an articulation too. The decluttering comes from simply not having the bandwidth for every bit of oxygen to the flame. We're not here to offer the free ride to the instigators of our violence. We have begun to see ourselves as too precious for all this. After all, the burden of being aflame is ours alone.

When we begin to feel the preciousness of our lives, when we see what a spectacular journey we are all on, how complex this flow of change we exist in is and how transitory each moment, we begin to value ourselves above all else.

We begin to value the present moment before it is gone.

The chase for the illusory goalpost is so distant and futile, the now so ephemeral, that we find the joy of existence in what we have when we have it. We are able to feel the firmness of the mountain, the collectiveness of the ocean, the expansiveness of the sky, the burn of the desires within our bodies and minds, and we become an ecosystem unto ourselves.

'The whole moon and the entire sky are reflected in one dewdrop on a blade of grass,' wrote Zen Master Dōgen Zenji. He uses the image to describe the perfect understanding of impermanence found in a state of meditation. The world and all its luminous glory is but a reflection in our transient bodies. To the dewdrop, its lifespan seems long.

Our infinitude is momentary, and in that is reflected everything we deem permanent.

The flame burns out the oxygen it has in the moment of its existence as new oxygen feeds the new flame. The flame you see is not the flame you began with. Both oxygen and flame die the moment they consume each other, passing the baton on to the new oxygen and the new flame. In each moment a passion, in each moment a flame. Both consume each other and move us on to the next one in a rapid succession of impermanence that gives the illusion of permanence. This is Sunyata.

We cannot exist in a future that is not here and that we will not know. We cannot live in a past that no longer exists.

If we exist, we exist now, in the moment, with what comes at us as input and how we experience it.

In the stillness is our awareness of the moment, complete in its potential.

This is how to be fire.

12

The Ember in the Forest

A YOUNG WOMAN FORAGING IN THE FOREST BUNDLED UP all the firewood she could carry on her head. She looked at the small pile of twigs that were too small to carry yet too many to waste. The afternoon was turning to evening and a chill was settling in, and she thought, 'Let me build a fire before I go.' She pulled out a matchbox from the folds of her sari and set them alight. As she sat on her haunches looking into the flames, she felt a sense of peace. She had a hard life – in-laws, husband and children to attend to, cooking, farm work, fetching water. This was the extent of her existence, her duties interminable and exhausting. She felt stuck. The change that came to others never seemed to come to her. She would have welcomed it. The only relief from this life, she believed, was death. As the flames danced she wondered if she would ever be happy. She began to pick up the dry leaves around her and naming each one for a desire she nurtured, a dream she once harboured, a love she once whispered, a talent she never used, and tossed them one by one into the flame. With each addition, she noticed, the flame shot a little bit higher. Encouraged, she found more leaves, more twigs and naming them for more hidden desires and resentments, she kept chanting and tossing them into the flame. The small bonfire was now a blazing wildfire. It went higher and higher and caught on overhanging branches; it danced from tree to tree until it had spread beyond the clearing. Thick black smoke poured forth and she had trouble breathing. She made her escape and ran towards the village to warn everyone. The villagers rushed back with her, carrying buckets of water and, after much battling, brought the flames under control. The young woman saw what had almost happened and was thankful the worst had not occurred. Night had fallen, and she had dinner to cook. She couldn't find the matchbox. She searched everywhere. She must have dropped it in the forest while fighting the blaze. She and her husband sat down and began to laugh. They laughed and they laughed until tears rolled down their cheeks. Then they borrowed a matchbox from the neighbour and made dinner. The next day, she went back to the forest to forage and retrieved her matchbox. She slipped it back into the folds of her sari and went about her day.

~

The way to control change is to use it. When we use it, we move with the wind and not against it. Obstacles on the path or diversions become corrections in our trajectory. We are constantly recalibrating where we want to go and how we will get there. We have told ourselves to persevere at any cost for so long that we are unwilling to question our goal, our path and our intentions. When everything else is fixed, the only available avenue is to blame others for what gets in our way. We fail to see that they too are buffeted by the same winds and flames. This is the gap of compassion. When we gain this lens, we will be able to see others suffering too. Their getting in our way will not feel as personal, and we can focus our energy on going around the obstacle they present. We can't sail across the ocean in a predetermined straight line. We will find ourselves slamming into rocks or other ships and damage both them and ourselves. We have to navigate the waters with the path as it opens up to us.

Here are five steps to use the change that comes to us in our lives:

1. TAME THE FLAME

Any good cook knows you don't start off a recipe with the highest flame. Turn it down, let the heat build, know when to simmer, when to roast, and when to cook on residual heat. Learning to control the flame is one of the least taught and most valuable life lessons. If everything inside us is a burn, is it any wonder we are constantly exhausted? We are not just providing the fuel for the fire, we are the fuel. When you work with a high fire, you are offering yourself up for consumption. Turn it down. A high flame is also what has the potential to go out of control. It inflicts damage on oneself as well as others. We want plentiful rain but we don't welcome a flood. More is not always beneficial for us. A low flame is one that we can control the use of. We channel, direct, regulate and rekindle it as per our need.

The flame meditation:

Close your eyes and sit comfortably but with your spine erect as far as possible. Observe your breath until you find its rhythm. Now begin to scan your body from the fontanelle to your toes by passing your attention over each and every part of your body. As you pass through your forehead, eyes, nose, neck, your arms, down the torso and back, past the genitals, to the thighs, knees and feet, observe any sensations that arise. Note in particular the ones that emanate heat, clenching, tightness, a burning sensation. Often this is on our overworked palms and fingers, the soles of the feet, the neck and throat, the tongue or the forehead. Observe where yours occur and note them down. As memories and thoughts come up, observe which ones generate heat in this way. Note where the sensation occurs. Each time you meditate observe if these sensations have gone up or down. Keep a heat diary over a period of time and see which parts of your body feel the burning and what sparks them. For instance, it could be: 'pit of the stomach – angry thoughts about my boss'. Each time you observe the sensation, you will begin to notice that you're becoming conscious of the trigger and you will be able to choose the action to respond with, rather than reacting to it. In time, the trigger will no longer have the power to elicit a response from you without your permission. This is how to lower the flame.

2. SET BOUNDARIES

The secret to regulating our fire lies in setting up a fence and a gate. This allows us to carefully measure and quantify what we allow into us and when. We are also able to check in with ourselves regularly, clean out the clutter, remove the stressors and aggravations, and ensure that little distracts us from it or adds to our inner fire without our knowledge. We do this to give us an authentic reading on what we are consuming, whether it is food or news, conversations or reading. When we have dogs or babies and we have to take them to the vet or doctor, one of the first questions we are asked is what they have been eating. And because we care for them, we are watching them and guarding them, we know the answer off the top of our heads. We do not seem to offer ourselves the same kindness. Further, we make a virtue of being open to everything and everyone. This is a romanticized idea of what an open life really means. When we are too open we are offering ourselves up for consumption. We have little value for our own time and energy. We are seeking the validation of others who let us know that we have been seen and heard. When we zealously guard our intake, protecting ourselves against too much of the negative and the positive, deprivation and indulgence, rejection and craving, we begin to lead a more balanced life. What we need comes into balance with what we get. In doing so, we move ourselves from the constant focus of meeting our own needs and free up the mind space to become more available to meet the needs of others, because we know we are taken care of. This makes us authentically more open than simply being a dustbin for the world of sensory input.

Watch me watch me diary:

Keep a diary that will allow you to watch you observing yourself. It will help to quantify the sensory input you allow yourself on a daily basis. Have these rows: listening, watching, speaking, tasting, touching. To begin with simply jot down one striking aspect of the day that occurred in each category. Add a column for the duration. Say, you watched the news, for one hour. Now add a column for the thoughts and feelings it left you with. So you could say 'inspired' or 'angry' or 'envious'. You could check in with this list once or twice a day, perhaps in the morning and evening, depending on how often you remember to do it. As you jot down the item, consider what it made you think and feel. How do you feel about having used an hour of your day on something that made you angry? As your observation of yourself grows, you will be able to consider habits that eat into your time and energy but contribute little to you. This will begin to free up energy and time for the things that will help you reach your goals. You will only need to keep this up until regulating and boundary setting becomes ingrained and a cultivated practice.

3. HAVE A DISCIPLINE

Your regulation of the flame and your boundary setting needs to exist within the framework of a discipline. Otherwise, it's just a fence with gaping holes in it through which the fox gets in. When you have a discipline to fall back on, ask any sportsman, some days you will feel like training and some days your body and mind just won't move. You go through the motions regardless, but it isn't futile – what you are doing is setting up an algorithm that will work without your intervention as you get used to it. The run you go on is still working on what it needs to work on whether or not you're enjoying it. I began to wake up at 4.30 a.m., initially to complete my personal writing before I went off to my journalism job. That job no longer exists, but I have become so accustomed to that routine that I wake up at the same time without an alarm. It has given me the space to read, meditate, work on my podcast or do anything else I may choose to. It opens up my day. Your practice doesn't have to be a popular one, or one that works for others. It simply has to work for you, and it has to be consistent. It's no help to meditate for one hour every 15 days, it's better to do silent sitting for 10 minutes every day. Pick your practice and fit it into your life in the way that works for you. This is your regulation mechanism and framework.

Token push system:
Let's say you pick a discipline. This could be intermittent fasting, meditating for half an hour, going for a walking meditation, silent sitting, an art hour, doodling, painting, music, whatever works for you. Now all you need to do is stick to it. Create a rewards system for your discipline. If it is silent sitting, link it to a treat, say, watching an episode of your favourite show. Now, you cannot watch your show until you've completed your silent sitting for the day. You could link it to social media time or a slice of cake, whatever tempts you enough to want to stick to the discipline. If it's possible, put in

an interruption app that sets a reminder. It also helps to have alarms and reminders set in your phone as well as put a family member in charge of urging you. Annoying teens can be very useful in this way. Tell them they get a reward every time they successfully get you to stick to the plan. Make it expensive enough that you begin to follow the plan without their reminders soon enough. You only need to do this as long as it takes you to overcome the inertia.

4. BE A GIVER

Give your time, give your energy, give your attention, give your money, give your skills, give your knowledge. Whatever you can give away, give it in as much quantities as you are able to. Note that this is after you have done the first three, which safeguard you and your inner work. Giving is often viewed as an act of charity. It is considered a luxury and a necessity to correct the balance of injustice in the world. That's one way of looking at it. The other is that those who give the most have the most. And the reason for this is they don't become bottlenecks of energy. They are standing in the confluence of their conditions and owning what comes at them. They become channels of easy passage. Like a gap between two mountains where the air rushes through, people who give find energy flowing towards them. Money, wealth, assets, food, people, knowledge, praise and blame, these are all manifestations of energy. People who give, whose gaze is outwards, are not being static and stagnant recipients. That's a one-way blast that will die out soon or come in bursts because the energy has no way to flow. They have cracked a code: the more you give the more comes at you. We don't always have much to give, we think, but we have all seen volunteers go at it even when they put themselves at risk. Give what you are able to, when you are able to, in terms of resources, time or energy. Put a handful of grain out for the birds or help a neighbour's kid with his homework, help fetch a senior citizen their groceries if that is all you can give, but include at least one way of giving in your day. It frees up the flows of energies and you benefit along with others. The more your gaze goes outwards, the lesser the hold your own problems have over you. Giving also bolsters your confidence. The giver is never in an inferior position, and we are all capable of giving. We just haven't explored all the ways in which we can give. The more you practise this, the more it will open up avenues for giving and receiving both. Many of us are also uncomfortable with receiving. The practice will also calibrate our response to receiving, which will become easier once we begin to give.

The outward gaze:

Simhasana, the lion pose, clears three major blocks – the root, the neck and the abdominal. It activates the feeling of being self-sufficient and powerful. It self-protectively directs the gaze outwards and opens the face. It releases tension, fear, anger and stress. It channels energy outwards.

Sit with your knees folded, in Vajrasana. Part your knees slightly and allow one ankle to cross over the other behind you. Gently press down on the ground in front of your knees with your palms, leaning forward over them such that your arms are straight. Keep your gaze soft and parallel to the floor, dropping your chin slightly to achieve this. Exhale deeply and stick your tongue out as far as it will go. Release a 'ha' sound that opens out your throat even more. Keep your attention on the spot between your brows.

5. RUTHLESSLY ALIGN

We are less afraid of change than of not knowing where we are headed and what we are subject to. Once we have befriended the unknown, a lot of the fear of uncertainty goes away, but we are still a bit all over the place. In order to walk on a new path, it is essential to move away from the detritus of the old one. This requires a decluttering, which can seem harsh. Let go of old ways of working, seeing, thinking and doing. Let go of the things that sucked out your time and energy. Let go of people who do not contribute to your focus. As you set boundaries, regulate your flame, find a discipline and give more of yourself, you will find that a lot of the old ways begin to drop away on their own. This is because you are turning. You are turning towards what feels more authentically like you. You are turning towards your true self.

Sometimes it is painful to let go of ideas, let alone people who have walked a long path with us when we were not so clear. However, staying in a relationship that provides no clarity for them or you is contributing harm to someone else's journey too. If you genuinely love someone, you want to see them move out of their own confusion, burn and find their fulfilment. And you need to ask if your actions are helping them do that. Sometimes, it takes a little while, but when people around you notice that the things you are doing benefit you, they come seeking too. So release what you have to do, both for yourself as well as for others around you.

As you ruthlessly realign, you will find yourself discarding the inauthentic, the time-wasters, the energy-suckers, the obstacles and path clutter. You will scold yourself for rejecting great opportunities in jobs and relationships that simply don't suit your purpose. Your purpose now has become far more important than the transient comings and goings of life. You will find your feet move forward slowly and steadily.

If the previous steps are working for you, you will find yourself realigning – physically, mentally, emotionally and spiritually – towards a purpose that is higher than what can be impacted by everyday change. You will find the opportunities you need open up, acceptance comes easier, collaborations work out, and you begin to connect with what and who you need to fulfil your journey.

You are now living a life of trust and openness.

You are now living your Impermanence.

Acknowledgements

This book would not have been possible without the refuge offered by S.N. Goenka and Dzongsar Khyentse Rinpoche. I am grateful for the quiet and kind mentoring of my teachers Ferzeen Faroodi, Sujata Abraham, Nirmala Almeida, Asha Pillai-Balsara, Nirmala Ganla, Amal Ghosh and Arne Schelling, as well as Neha and Nabhiraj. I thank my cohorts at Mind & Temple, and WCCLF (Pune), at St Xavier's Institute of Counselling Psychology (Mumbai), and in my Vipassana groups. Dr Mamatha Shetty for temperance; Mimansa Popat, Dhara Shah, and Hiral Mehta for their generous ear and wisdom. Kim D'Souza, my sounding board. Amish Tripathi and Bhavna Roy for unerring friendship and shelter. Madhu and Priya for solidity.

What is possible even without Kanishka? Our cosy team at Hachette: publisher Poulomi Chatterjee, who is such a strong undercurrent to this book; editor Swarnima Narayan, who edits like a stealth bomber; in marketing, Sohela Singh with her wide-reaching vision; and Cibani Premkumar and Aditi Nichani, who helped me conceive this.

Not least, my parents, Laxmi and Jayaraman, for encouraging everything; siblings, Gauri and Gautam; and my absolute rocks, Ramesh and Kalpana. Anushka for her consideration. Zitto, for Zen that transcends humans. And above all, Dhruv.